Risk Awareness and Corporate Governance

Brian Coyle

institute of
financial services

Financial World Publishing

IFS House

4-9 Burgate Lane

Canterbury

Kent

CT1 2XJ

United Kingdom

T   01227 812012

F   01227 479641

E   editorial@ifslearning.com

W   www.ifslearning.com

Financial World Publishing publications are published by The Chartered Institute of Bankers, a non-profit making registered educational charity.

The Chartered Institute of Bankers believes that the sources of information upon which the book is based are reliable and has made every effort to ensure the complete accuracy of the text. However, neither CIB, the author nor any contributor can accept any legal responsibility whatsoever for consequences that may arise from errors or omissions or any opinion or advice given.

Typeset by Kevin O'Connor

Printed by Ashford Colour Press Ltd

© Chartered Institute of Bankers 2002

ISBN 0-85297-667-4

CONTENTS

Contents

INTRODUCTION

The concept of this book

This study text has been written for students of The Chartered Institute of Bankers' DFSM module Risk Awareness and Corporate Governance and for practitioners in financial services who are looking for a practical refresher.

Each chapter is divided into sections and contains learning objectives and clear, concise topic-by-topic coverage.

Syllabus

The key sections of the Risk Awareness and Corporate Governance syllabus are:

● The nature and concept of Risk

● Assessment

● Analysis

● Control of Risk

● Containment of Risk

● Background Company Law

● Directors

● Good Practice

Your contribution

Although this study text is designed to stand alone, as with most topics certain aspects of this subject are constantly changing. Therefore it is very important that you keep up-to-date with these key areas. For example, you should read the quality press and financial journals and look out for relevant websites.

We anticipate that you will study this course for one session (six months), reading through and studying approximately one unit every week. However, note that as topics vary in size and as knowledge tends not to fall into uniform chunks, some units are unavoidably longer than others.

Study plan

If you are a distance-learning student and have not received your study plan by the beginning of the session, please contact the **ifs** Student Learning Support Department.

Tel: 01227 818637

Fax: 01227 453547

e-mail: sls@ifslearning.com

1

THE NATURE AND CONCEPT OF RISK

After reading this chapter, you should:

- Understand the nature and concept of risk
- Be aware of the scope of risk management
- Understand how risks might be classified
- Be aware that risk has a cost
- Be aware of the potential consequences of ignoring or not recognizing risk.

1.1   Defining risk

Risk is a concept that we all understand, or at least think that we can do, but it is not easily defined.

- Risk is often associated with the possibility that something harmful or damaging could occur if things go wrong, resulting in physical injury, loss or damage to possessions, a legal liability or a financial loss. These risks are higher when the situation makes it more likely that an adverse event will occur. For example, the risk of physical injury is higher for individuals in a situation where the possibility of an injury is high, such as for individuals who play contact sports, parachute out of aeroplanes or go rock climbing.

- Risk is also associated with taking a chance or a gamble, where the outcome could be either favourable or adverse. An individual who goes to a casino hopes to win money, but could lose money or might break even.

- A third aspect of risk arises from the fact that the actual outcome of an event or situation could differ from what was expected or planned for. For example, a person might plan a summer holiday hoping for hot weather and expecting the temperature to be around 25 degrees Celsius, only to find that the actual weather is either much hotter or much cooler than expected.

Risk exists for businesses as well as individuals. It could be argued that when companies collapse, they do so because they have failed to manage their risk properly. Some risks are unavoidable, and the profits earned by a business can be seen as a reward for the risks that it takes. On the other hand, some risks might be unnecessary and avoidable. Other risks might be reduced, but at a cost. Risk management is concerned with identifying, assessing and controlling the risks facing a business, and with incorporating risk issues into decision-making processes.

Risk can be defined as the possible variation in an outcome from what is expected to happen. This definition of risk contains three important elements.

- Risk is about variability.

- Risk relates to our expectations of what will happen.

- Risk relates to the difference between what we expect to happen, and what the actual outcome might be.

Pure risk and speculative risk

There are two types of risk.

- **Downside risk** or **pure risk** is the possibility either that the outcome will be what we expect, or that something bad will happen and a loss will occur. It is the risk of something going wrong. An individual does not expect to be involved in an accident, to become seriously ill, or to suffer fire, flooding or a burglary in the home. However, these things could happen. The management of pure risk or downside risk is often associated with taking out **insurance** policies, and claiming on the policy when an adverse event occurs, to recover the loss suffered.

- **Two-way risk** or **speculative risk** arises when the actual outcome could be either better or worse than expected. We might have an expectation of what will happen, but the actual outcome could turn out either better or worse. Speculative risk arises naturally in business, where trading results could turn out better or worse than expected, and so profits could be higher or lower. Speculative risk could be associated with taking a gamble. More commonly in business, the management of two-way risk is more concerned with putting the organization into a position where it can respond to unexpected developments, on order to minimize the losses from an adverse situation or to exploit favourable opportunities that arise.

The sources of risk and exposure to risk

Risk has a source. For example, one source of the risk of road accidents is bad weather, causing bad visibility and dangerous road conditions. Bad weather is also a source of the risk of flooding and damage to houses. In business, risk can arise out of not using the most recent technology, having inadequately trained employees or failure to control costs. Each of these risks could have an adverse effect on customer attitudes, sales volumes and profitability.

Some risk factors give rise to two-way risk. For example, foreign exchange rates could move up or down, affecting companies that export or import goods or services. The economy could enter a growth phase or go into recession, with the result that customer demand for a company's services or products might rise or fall. The business outcome could be either better or worse than expected, and give rise to opportunities as well as threats.

An individual or a business is affected by risk only if there is **exposure** to it. An individual is not affected by the risk of an air crash if he or she avoids air travel. Similarly, a business will not be affected by changes in the economy of an emerging market country if it does no business with that country. The size of a risk varies with the size of the exposure. For example, all businesses are affected by variability in the price of crude oil, because oil prices affect energy prices and fuel prices. Some businesses are more exposed to oil price risk than others, and so face a larger risk. Exposure creates the motivation to act to control or contain a risk. Taking measures to limit or avoid risk is sometimes known as **hedging** the risk or hedging the exposure. The idea of hedging is that the risk should be contained within a certain boundary or limit.

Risks for companies and risks for investors

The risks facing a company can be looked at from the point of view of either the company itself or its investors. Risks facing a company are factors that give rise to variable profits or unexpected losses. For example, there is the risk that sales demand from customers will be disappointing, or that a new product will have an unsuccessful market launch, or that there will be a shortage of skilled labour. Risk assessment should be a part of the management decision-making process, particularly for long-term capital investment decisions. The risk of losses could also arise from inadequate financial controls, which could expose the business to fraud or the possibility of unauthorized financial spending or financial commitments.

It is important to recognize that companies cannot avoid risks, because by its very nature, business involves some risk. However, unnecessary risks should be avoided, and the risks taken on by a company should be consistent with the nature of its operations and the size of the returns it expects to make. Management needs to decide what level of risks is acceptable, and how risks should be controlled.

The risk for investors in a company is that the returns they receive will be less than expected. In an extreme case, there is the risk of losing the entire investment if the company becomes insolvent. Bondholders in a company are exposed to a risk that the company will be unable to meet its obligations to pay interest or repay the debt principal when the bonds mature. Investors will demand a higher rate of return (ie a higher rate of interest) from a higher-risk credit, as compensation for taking on the extra risk.

The ordinary shareholders bear the ultimate risk in a company. The dividends they receive are dependent on what the company can afford to pay them, which in turn depends on the profits the company has made and the strength of its cash flows. When expectations of future profits take a turn for the worse, shareholders will suffer from a fall in the market price of their shares. When a company becomes insolvent and goes into liquidation, the equity shareholders rank last in order of priority for repayment, and will not recover any of their investment unless all the creditors of the company have first been paid in full what they are owed.

In this text, the focus of attention is on risks for companies, and the management of those risks.

1.2   Risk management

A brief history of risk management

Risk management had its origins with the insurance of risks. Organizations wishing to offload certain risks can take out insurance policies, such as buildings insurance, equipment insurance, employee liability insurance, and so on. For large companies, the negotiation of insurance policies, and the process of making claims under insurance policies, can be both complex and time-consuming. Companies might therefore employ specialist risk managers to do the work.

The cost of insurance premiums varies according to the nature of the risk. Preventative measures to reduce risks can therefore reduce the cost of insurance. For example, the risk of losses from fire damage to a building can be reduced by installing a sprinkler system, and the risk of physical injury to employees can be reduced by providing protective clothing. Action to reduce risks should result in lower premium costs for insurance policies. The managers appointed to arrange insurance cover have become involved in measures to reduce the insured risks, such as health and safety at work and engineering risks, in order to reduce costs.

As the understanding of insurable risks developed, some large organizations began to question whether buying insurance was the best option, and whether it might be better financially for the organization to bear certain risks itself.

Another strand in the development of risk management has been the role of accountants (and financial control systems) and auditors. All businesses face the risk of losses due to fraud or to lax procedures and financial controls. A different aspect of risk management is the task of ensuring that the organization's system of internal controls to prevent fraud and to safeguard the business assets. Traditionally, this task has commonly been undertaken by external or internal auditors.

Yet another strand of risk management emerged in the 1970s with developments in the understanding of financial risks, and techniques for controlling those risks. Many financial risks are speculative (two-way) risks for which insurance policies are not usually appropriate. For some companies, particularly banks, forward contracts and derivative instruments such as swaps and options have evolved as a method of hedging financial risks.

Risk management continues to evolve. More recently, in countries such as the USA and the UK, risk management has become a central issue of corporate governance. It is recognized that, in order to survive, companies need to be aware of all the significant risks they face, and should have a system in place for controlling them. There should be an enterprise-wide and integrated approach to risk management. In the UK, for example, listed companies are required to review their risk management systems regularly, and report to shareholders annually.

The risk manager

Risk management continues to develop and grow in importance. Directors of large public companies, for example, now see regular risk reports and assessments of risk performance.

Risk managers tend to focus on 'operational risk' and contingency planning, although some organizations have specialist types of risk manager, such as credit risk managers in banks. Effective risk management is all about getting business managers to assume ownership of the management of risks within their own areas. Contingency planning and crisis management planning includes incident management, public relations, relocation and disaster recovery in many situations, from product recall to the loss of strategic staff, a major pollution incident or even a terrorist attack.

In banking, protection of IT facilities and fraud avoidance are part of the risk manager's role, and this task is carried out in close collaboration with the internal audit department.

Corporate governance requirements, described in more detail in a later chapter, are encouraging large companies to review the role of their audit committee and ask whether the committee's brief should be extended to include risk management, or whether a separate risk management committee should be established, reporting to the board.

Delimiting risk

Delimiting risk means setting a boundary or limit to risks. An organization needs to know how big are the risks that it faces and how much of this risk can safely be tolerated. Managers should identify what are the risks facing their organization, and how much they might cost. A useful starting point is to understand the nature of different risks by classifying or categorizing them.

1.3 Classifications of risk

Classifying risks can help with identifying and delimiting the major risks facing an organization. Risks of a similar type might also be similarly managed. Generally speaking, risks are classified according to their source or characteristics, but there is no accepted 'official' system of classification.

A distinction is often made between business risk and non-business risk. **Business risks** for a company are the risks arising from the nature of its business and its operations, and out of business conditions. Business risks are generally two-way risks, and include product risk, macro-economic risk and technology risk.

- *Product risk* arises from the possibility that customers will not buy the products or services of a company in the expected quantities. The demand for an existing product might drop unexpectedly, perhaps because a competitor develops a better rival version. A new product launched on to the market might fail to win the anticipated customer interest.

- *Macro-economic risk* (or economic risk) refers to the effect on a company's business of unexpected changing economic conditions. When the economy stagnates or enters a recession, consumer demand for goods and services will fall, and companies generally will suffer from the slow-down. On the other hand, when the economy picks up, all companies should expect to benefit from improving business conditions.

- *Technology risk* arises when a market or industry is affected by some change in technology, affecting either the type or design of products that companies provide or the methods they use to make them or deliver them to customers. There are numerous examples of companies being forced to respond to unexpected developments in technology. Just one such example has been the response of commercial banks to Internet technology. In the UK all retail banks offer Internet banking, but still face the risks (downside risks and upside potential) of further technological developments in the future

There are also speculative risks in business. These include the risks from choosing one particular business strategy rather than another (*strategy risk*). The term *enterprise risk* refers to the success or failure of a business operation, and whether it should have been undertaken in the first place. When a company is planning a major new venture, for example if it is planning a takeover bid for another company, enterprise risk would refer to the possibility that the acquisition will be financially unsuccessful.

Within the broad category of business risks are various pure risks. *Property/casualty risks* ('p/c risks') are those where the business is exposed to either loss of property or losses arising from accidents. These include health and safety risks, risks of losses arising as a consequence of employee behaviour (employee liability risks), engineering risk and IT security risk. Many companies, particularly those in manufacturing, often face risks arising from failure to deal properly with *environmental risks* such as the consequences of pollution.

Non-business risk is any type of risk other than business risk. Many non-business risks are classified as either financial risks or event risks.

Financial risk arises from factors external to the business, and of a financial nature. Financial risks, many of which are two-way risks, can be classified according to the source of the risk.

- *Credit risk* refers to the possibility that creditors of the business will fail to pay what they owe in full and on time ('default risk') or that a company will suffer a downgrading of its credit rating.

- *Foreign exchange risk* refers to the possibility of making unexpected gains or losses from changes in a foreign exchange rate. For example, if a UK firm has a dollar bank account containing $1,000,000, it will make a gain if the dollar strengthens in value against sterling, and make a loss if the dollar weakens in value.

- *Interest rate risk* arises from the consequences of any unexpected change in interest rates. For individuals, one example of interest rate risk is the possibility of a change in the mortgage rate. Companies are also likely to be affected by changes in interest rates.

- *Market risk* is a general term for the risk of an adverse movement in market prices, which could be foreign exchange rates or interest rates, but, in a financial context, more commonly refers to the risk of changes in the market price of shares and bonds.

- *Liquidity risk* has two aspects. One element of liquidity risk, also known as *cash-flow risk*, refers to the possibility of an unexpected shortage of cash, which could result in an inability to pay obligations when they fall due or even insolvency unless additional sources of liquidity (such as extra borrowing) can be found. The second element of liquidity risk refers to the possibility that a transaction cannot be made at the current market prices because the size of the transaction is either too large or too small relative to the normal acceptable size of trading 'lots'. For example, an investor wanting to sell an unusually large quantity of shares in company X, a small quoted company, might find that there is no one prepared to buy the shares except at a price far below the current market price of the shares.

- Companies dealing in commodities face *commodity price risk*, which is the possibility of higher-than-expected or lower-than-expected commodity prices.

- For non-financial companies, *gearing risk* refers to the risks of high borrowing in relation to the amount of shareholders' capital in the business. A high level of debt ('high gearing') increases the risk of both volatility in earnings per share and also, when debt levels are very high, of insolvency due to an inability to meet debt repayment schedules.

- For banks, *capital adequacy risk* refers to the possibility that a bank will have insufficient capital to support its volume of business, as required by capital adequacy regulations.

Operational risk might be included as a category of financial risk, or regarded as a separate category of risk. There is no widely-accepted definition of operational risk. It might be defined narrowly to mean errors in operations arising from human or technological errors. It can also be defined more broadly to meet all the risks of direct and indirect losses from failed or inadequate processes and systems, both from human errors and from external events. Operational risks might be treated as a category of financial risks because many of the risks are monitored and controlled through internal control systems, and subject to investigation by internal or external auditors.

Event risks arise from negative events that are either largely or entirely outside the control of the organization. All of them are downside risks, against which it might be possible to obtain third party insurance. Event risk includes:

- *Litigation risk.* This is the risk that someone will make a claim against the organization through legal action. In some businesses, such as the tobacco industry, litigation risk can be very high.

- *Disaster risk* refers to the possibility that an unexpected catastrophe might occur, adversely affecting the organization. These include the risks of fire damage, flooding, ill health of key executives, terrorist attacks, and so on.

- *Regulatory and political risk* arises from the possibilities that unexpected new laws or regulations might be introduced, affecting the business and profitability of an organization.

- A threat to a business can also arise from *reputational risk*, where the activities of a firm could damage its reputation in the eyes of customers.

Classifying risks by their environmental source

Another way of classifying risks is according to the environmental source from which they originate.

- Risks in the *physical environment* relate to matters such as climate and geology.

- Risks in the *social environment* relate to changes in tastes and attitudes, and to demographic changes.

- Risks in the *political environment* relate to the changes arising from decisions by the government, or a change of government.

- Risks in the *legal environment* arise from changes in legislation and regulations, or from the consequences of breaching the law, or failing to fulfil duties or obligations imposed by the law.

- Changes in the *general economic environment* can also give rise to risks.

- There are also risks in the *operational environment* in which an organization carries out its activities.

Risk and uncertainty

Risk is often associated with uncertainty. Risk arises out of the variability in a situation, whereas **uncertainty** is in the mind. For example, the actual outcome of an event might be A or B, with a 50% probability of each outcome. The risk in the situation is that either outcome might occur, but the risk is measurable and understood. However, an individual might be unaware that only outcomes A and B are possible, or might be unaware of the probabilities of the two possible outcomes. Uncertainty arises from a lack of information and, in business, it could result in taking decisions without all the relevant facts. Uncertainty can be reduced by obtaining more or better information. Better information, by reducing uncertainty, should improve the quality of decision-making, even though the risk itself is not affected by understanding more about it.

1.4   The cost of risk

Risk has a cost or value. For pure risk that is uninsured, its cost is the amount of the loss if an adverse outcome were to occur. If the loss is wholly insured, its cost is the total insurance premiums payable over the insurance period. Where the risk is only partly hedged, the cost of the risk is a combination of the loss that would occur in the event of an adverse outcome plus the cost of constructing the hedge.

Suppose for example that a company wants to insure its five properties against flood damage, and it has been estimated that if damage were to occur to any property, the cost would be

£100,000. An insurance company has estimated that the risk of flood damage to the properties is 1 in 20 each year. The insurance premium would therefore be at least £25,000 per year to cover all five properties (1/20 x £100,000 x 5 properties). If the estimate of the insurance company is correct, there will be flood damage to one of the five properties about once every four years, and an annual premium of £25,000 would just about cover the insurance claim. In practice, the premium would have to be higher, to allow for the administration costs of the insurance company and for a profit margin.

The point to note in this example is that insurance is not so much a way of avoiding loss as a way of spreading the cost of the risk. If losses could avoided altogether through insurance, the insurance companies themselves would be loss-making. The cost of loss can therefore be assessed without considering insurance premiums: it is the amount of the loss if an adverse event were to occur. The annual cost of a risk is the amount of the loss if an adverse event were to occur multiplied by the probability of it occurring in any year.

Cost of loss = Amount of loss x Probability

The cost of speculative or two-way risk arises from the volatility or variability in possible outcomes. Greater volatility increases the risk, and when risk is higher, investors should require a bigger return. The cost of speculative risk is the loss of value arising as a consequence of the risk. Suppose that there are two companies X and Y, each of which pays out all its profits each year in dividends to shareholders. Company X has no risks and will make a profit of £200,000 each year. Company Y has some risk, and there is a 50% chance that it will make a profit of £400,000 and a 50% chance that it will just break even and make no profit at all. The expected value of the profit of company Y is £200,000 (50% x £400,000 + 50% x £0), the same as company X. Shareholders in company X are certain to receive dividends of £200,000 each year, whereas shareholders in company Y will receive £400,000 in some years but nothing in others. Company Y shareholders have a higher speculative risk, and to compensate them for this risk, they will expect a higher return on their investment. As a consequence, the value of shares in company Y will be lower than the value of shares in company X.

A simple mathematical illustration might help to clarify this point. The value of a constant annual amount in perpetuity can be expressed by the equation:

$$V = c/r$$

Where V is the value of the annual cash flows in perpetuity, c is the amount of the annual cash flow and r is the required annual return on investment, expressed as a proportion or a percentage.

Returning to the example of company X and company Y. Suppose investors in company X require a return of 8% each year, and shareholders in company Y, where the speculative risk is higher, expect a higher annual return of 10%. Given an expected average annual profit and dividend of £200,000, the value of the shares in company X would be £2,500,000 (£200,000/0.08) and the value of the shares in company Y would be just £2,000,000 (£200,000/0.10). The cost of the extra risk in company Y is therefore £500,000.

1.5   How risk affects business

Risk affects business because it either reduces returns or creates greater volatility in returns. Either way, risk affects the value of the business. There is a trade-off between risk and returns. Some businesses offer low risk and comparatively low returns. Others offer higher returns for higher risk. A problem for both companies and investors is to achieve a suitable balance between expected returns and risk (volatility in those returns).

In some cases where the risk is severe, an unfavourable outcome might even threaten the financial viability of the business. This could occur, for example, if a new competitor enters the market with a better-quality and lower-priced product, or if there is a slump in customer demand due to a collapse in the economy, or if the company becomes so heavily indebted and short of cash that it cannot pay its creditors.

One aspect of risk management is to assess how each significant risk would affect the business, and devise appropriate control measures.

Perceptions of risk

Perceptions of risk are how the risk is seen and assessed. Risk perception is particularly well-developed in the banking and insurance markets, and in some cases, risk is measured or rated. In the bond markets, issues of corporate bonds are given a credit rating by specialist agencies such as Moody's and Standard & Poor's. The rating is then kept under review throughout the life of the bond, and adjusted if necessary. When giving a rating to bonds, a credit rating agency assesses the probability of default by the borrower. The perceived credit standing of a company is therefore judged by its credit rating, and the financial markets refer to companies as 'triple-A rated', 'investment grade', 'speculative grade', and so on.

Many banks use financial models to assess the risks that exist in their current business. A Value at Risk (VaR) model, for example, measures the amount of daily losses that a bank could incur, at a given level of probability. For example, a bank might be able to assess that there is a 5% probability that it could lose £10 million or more in a day on the trading or lending positions it has taken.

Investors often look at risk in terms of the trade-off with expected returns. Some companies are generally seen as 'high risk' and some are 'low risk'. A high-yield investment is one in which the expected returns are high to compensate or greater volatility in earnings or a higher risk of insolvency. Risk can be seen as a value proposition to investors. Risk should be managed and systems for monitoring and controlling risk should be in place. Some risks might be avoided, and some mitigated. The company will be left, however, with a residual risk. This is the total of the business risks and financial risks to which the company will be exposed. Investors in the company must accept these risks when choosing to buy its shares or bonds. This portfolio of risks is sometimes referred to as the company's value proposition to its investors. The value of the company's shares will be determined by the returns that management are able to provide, relative to the risks.

The subjective perception of risk

From a financial or economic perspective, risk has a potential cost, arising from a combination of the expected size of a loss or gain and the variability of possible outcomes around the expected value. Economic business decisions can therefore be taken by management with regard to both the expected amount of risk as well as the expected size of the return.

An alternative approach to analysing risk-based decisions is to consider a risk from the perspective of human perception. Slovic, Fischhoff and Lichtenstein (*Facts and Fears: Understanding Perceived Risk*, 1980) suggested that there are two other important aspects of a risk that affect our perceptions of it:

- The fear factor, which is how must we dread the potential outcome if the 'worst' actually happens.

- The control factor, which is the extent to which we are in control of events, and can take action to deal with the risk when it materializes.

When the fear factor is high and the control factor is low, a risk is perceived as being very great, and might therefore be avoided at all costs. For example, in the aftermath of the terrorist attacks in the USA on 11 September 2001, many American citizens would not fly, considering the risk too great. They feared the possibility of being on a high-jacked plane, knowing they would be powerless to do anything should an attack occur.

Perceptions of the current state of loss or gain affect the extent to which a person might seek or avoid risk. Kahneman and Tversky (1979) developed 'prospect theory', which is that different people make different choices under different conditions when faced with risk. When a person is in a position of gain, he becomes increasingly risk-averse and is less inclined to gamble because he wants to hold on to his gains. A person in a position of loss becomes more risk-seeking because he does not have much to lose. This asymmetry applies to attitudes to financial risk, but also to other risks as well, such as reputation risk.

Attitude to risk is also affected by a person's individual personality, and his or her inborn dispositions, feelings, biases and characteristics. Risk management decisions are therefore often based on a consensus view (or agreed policy) of what should be done about the risk, although individual managers will inevitably have different personal views about what should be done in different situations. For example, when faced with a decision about making a high-risk investment, some individual managers might argue against it, preferring to avoid the risk, whereas others might consider the risk worth undertaking to try to achieve the potential benefits.

1.6   The dangers of not recognizing risk

Risks can be significant in a changing business environment, and increase as the pace of change speeds up. New risks can arise, just as existing risks can become less severe or disappear altogether.

If management ignores risk or fails to recognize a major risk, the company will suffer an unexpected fall in profits. In the case of insurable risks, taking out an insurance premium spreads the cost of the risk evenly over time, whereas if the risk is not insured, profits will suffer a set-back in any year that an adverse event actually occurs.

One inevitable consequence of an unexpected fall in earnings for a stock-market company will be a sharp fall in its share price. You can verify this point by keeping an eye on financial news reports. Whenever a company announces a profit warning, or worse-than-expected results, the share price invariably falls. A second consequence of a fall in earnings could be a fall in the credit standing of the company. In some cases, the financial markets might question the ability of the company to continue in existence in its present form, and speculation might grow about a possible takeover bid. Companies with bank loans might be at risk of a breach in a loan covenant after a sharp fall in profits, and might therefore be required to renegotiate the terms of their loans.

A number of high-profile company collapses in recent years have been blamed on inadequate risk management. There have been many examples. In the UK, the financial difficulties of Marconi in 2001 could be attributed largely to strategic risk, and the company's exposure to a decline in the telecommunications industry, after having selected a strategy of investment in telecommunications. In the USA, the collapse of energy trader Enron in 2001 appears to have been attributable, to a large extent, to excessive financial exposures on trading positions.

Events can always turn out worse than expected. Management needs to understand, however, just how bad the outcome could be, and either control the risk by taking measures to insure against it or hedge it in other ways, or to have a contingency plan in case of emergency or necessity.

The risk environment is dynamic, and management must be on the look-out continually for new risks and changes in the significance of existing risks. Just one example might provide a useful illustration. The terrorist attack on New York on 11 September 2001 revealed a flaw in the contingency plans of several investment banks operating in the lower Manhattan financial district. Certain banks had extensive office accommodation within a localized 'campus' area, on the same telecommunications and power grids, which were put out of operation by the attack. The banks therefore found that they were unable to switch staff from damaged or destroyed buildings to other offices in the area. The risk of such a devastating terrorist attack in New York was recognized to an extent that had not been apparent before. It was reported some months later that two major investment banks were responding to the new risk environment by moving some major operations out of New York City.

The COCA concept and risk recognition

Although this text deals mainly with the analysis and control of existing risks, it is important to recognize that risk analysis should also be a part of the decision-making process. COCA stands for contracts, obligations, commitments and agreements, and the COCA concept is that a business organization can be seen as a collection of these, building up towards the achievement of the company's objectives.

Contracts are legally-enforceable agreements with another party, such as a customer, supplier or employee.

Obligations are also legally-binding but do not involve a contract. Typically, they arise out of laws or regulations, such as laws on health and safety at work, laws on pollution control, and so on.

Commitments are voluntary undertakings by an organization. Although there is no legal imperative, an organization might give a public commitment. For example, a supermarket or department store chain might advertise a commitment to offer the lowest prices on certain lines of consumer goods.

Agreements might be legally-binding contracts, but the term is also used to mean voluntary arrangements into which an organization enters. Agreements should be within the law, but could breach the law. A price cartel, where a group of rival producers collude to maintain the market price of their products, is such an example.

Whenever a company enters a new contract, is given a new obligation, or makes a new commitment or agreement, risks are created. Some of the risks could be significant, affecting the future profitability or financial stability of the organization. An evaluation of the risk should be considered before any contract, commitment or agreement is made.

1.7   A risk-based approach to management

Management can deal with risk in either of two ways (or by using a combination of the two). One approach is procedural, using a system of rules, regulations and procedures. Many measures for controlling the risk of fraud and safeguarding business assets are based on procedures such as authorizations, confirmations, double-checking, the use of passwords, and so on. It is essentially a defensive approach to risk control, and taken to extremes, procedural controls can become bureaucratic.

'Risk-based management' is an alternative approach that provides a focus for much of this text. It is broader in scope and more flexible in application than a procedural approach. It is based on continual reviews of the risks facing the business, through a process of identifying risks, assessing their potential impact, prioritizing them and devising ways of controlling those that appear significant. The responsibility for implementing risk control measures is assigned to appropriate individuals, who should then monitor and report their effectiveness.

The benefits of applying effective risk management and a system of internal control are as follows:

● A company can gain first-mover advantage by recognizing and responding to change before its rivals. In the medium-to-long term, this should give the company a strategic competitive advantage, and a dominant position in its market.

● Unexpected shocks are less likely to occur, because many eventualities should have been foreseen, and where appropriate countermeasures taken or contingency plans drawn up. Less management time should be spent on fire-fighting, which is a process of containing losses rather than creating profits.

- Risk management provides a good foundation for setting strategy. Consideration of how to deal with the risks facing a company should increase the probability of achieving the corporate objectives. There is also a greater likelihood that new initiatives will succeed, because more thought will have been given to what could go wrong, and contingency measures taken accordingly.

Risk management is not just about bad things happening. It is also about good things not happening, and missed opportunities. The following chapters go through stages in a risk-based management approach.

2

RISK ASSESSMENT

At the end of this chapter, you should:

- Understand the attitudes that companies and individuals might adopt towards risk

- Understand and be able to explain risk identification techniques

- Be aware of which individuals within an organization are responsible for risk management.

Introduction

A risk-based approach to management involves a continual cycle of assessing, analysing, controlling and containing risks. Ideally, this process should be embedded into the management systems of the organization, and be a part of its culture.

The assessment of risk is the first stage in the cycle, calling for both the identification of risks and an understanding of risk attitudes.

2.1   Corporate attitudes towards risk

A company's attitude towards risk determines the extent to which its management will take on risks in order to achieve the corporate objectives. 'Appetite' for risk refers to the willingness of an organization to take on risks. Avoiding risks or minimizing risks is not necessarily desirable, because a cautious approach will usually result in low returns on capital.

A company is not human and so its attitude to risk is a reflection of the attitudes of its management. Individual managers are most unlikely to share the same attitudes, and some will be more willing than others to take risks in the expectation of making higher profits and returns on investment. Where one manager might argue in favour of undertaking a new investment project, another might urge caution.

The attitude of a company towards risk can nevertheless be implied from the leadership given by its board of directors and from its corporate aims and strategies. These set out what objectives the company is trying to achieve, and the strategies it is adopting to achieve them. Some aims are more challenging than others, and a company that sets its ambitions high will have to take greater risks to achieve them. Similarly, some strategies are more risky than others.

It might help to consider a hypothetical example. Suppose there are two companies in the retail industry, each with a large chain of stores in the UK. Both companies are concerned about a slowdown in sales growth. One company might set as its aim the target of increasing revenues and profits by five per cent each year for the next five years, based on a strategy of opening a small number of new stores in the UK and diversifying its product range. The other company might set a target for sales and profits growth of twenty per cent each year for the next five years, based on a strategy of buying a retailing company in the USA. Both companies must accept some risk in order to achieve their aims, but the strategy of expansion into the USA, whether successful or not, will be more risky than a strategy of expanding the product range in existing markets. Management decisions taken by each company will then have to reflect the risk attitude inherent within its strategy.

Attitudes to risk might alter. A company might be forced to reassess its attitude when a new risk or opportunity emerges. The rapid development of Internet technology is an example. During the 1990s, corporate use of e-mail and Internet/intranet technology developed very rapidly, and predictions were made that private use of the Internet by individuals would increase to the point where existing technologies became obsolete. Within retail banking, for example, there were concerns that Internet banking would replace banking through branches. Banks were forced to assess the risk and opportunities created by Internet technology, and develop an Internet strategy. One option was to make Internet banking available to customers who wanted it, within the constraint of retaining most of the branch banking system. A strategy with much greater risk would have been to market Internet banking aggressively, encourage customers to make much less use of the branch banking system and seek ways of reducing significantly the number of branches. However, there would have been strong political pressure from the government discouraging banks from doing this, because individuals without a computer or an Internet connection would have been unable to use the new banking service. The choice of Internet strategy depended largely on the corporate attitude to risk, and not surprisingly, most banks have chosen a fairly cautious approach, investing heavily in the new technology but partly for defensive reasons, to build up an Internet capability similar to those of rival banks.

Investors assess the attitude of a company towards risk from its stated aims and strategies. Investors have their own attitudes to risk, and will seek to build up an investment portfolio that reflects their expectations of risk and return. An investor wanting to accept some risk in the hope of obtaining higher returns will identify and invest in companies with a high-risk strategy.

Risk management is not simply about reducing or eliminating risks. The aim should be to achieve a balanced portfolio of risks that support the company's aims and strategies. Risk should be kept within limits that are consistent with those aims and strategies.

2.2 Individual attitudes to risk

In practice, it is simply not possible to define a company's attitude to risk in specific measured terms. Within the framework of the company's overall aims and strategies, specific decisions are taken, either by individual managers or by management teams. Managers should consider the risk factor when making their decisions, and the availability of good-quality risk information will help to reduce the uncertainty in their decision-making. However, even if managers can reach the same understanding of a particular risk, their individual attitudes to the risk will differ. Important decisions will often be made only after extensive arguments, and by reaching a consensus or a compromise.

Differences in attitude are unavoidable. However, an aim of risk management should be to encourage managers to discuss both risk and their attitudes to risk. Managers might agree on the nature and size of the risk, but have differing attitudes towards it, what should be done about it, or whether the risk is worth accepting given the potential size of the returns. In other words, managers might agree on the possible outcomes from a decision, but disagree as to whether the risk is worth taking. Within the decision-making process, an awareness of differing attitudes and why they exist, and a willingness to discuss risk, should help management to reach a consensus.

Risk averse attitude

Management should consider both the risk and the expected return when making decisions, and the decision will be influenced by the risk attitude of the decision-maker. When there are a number of mutually exclusive options, each option might offer a different combination of risk and return. The problem is then to choose the preferred option.

An attitude is said to be *risk-averse* when the decision-maker will prefer an option offering the same return (or a higher return) for a lower risk, or an option offering a higher return for the same risk (or a lower risk).

Suppose that there are four mutually exclusive options, and management has to decide which of the options to select. For each one, there is an expected return on capital and an assessment of the risk. This risk has been measured statistically as a potential variation in the expected return.

Option	Expected return	Risk
	%	%
A	8	5
B	9	6
C	9	5
D	10	7

In this example, a risk-averse decision-maker will reach the following conclusions.

- He will prefer option C to option A, because it offers a higher expected return for the same risk.

- He will also prefer option C to option B, because it offers the same expected return for a lower risk.

- Option D offers a higher expected return than option C but a higher risk. Option C has the lower return, but the lower risk. The decision-maker might select either option, because, to his way of thinking, neither is clearly preferable to the other.

2.3 Identifying risks

A risk-based approach to management starts with identifying what the risks are and understanding them. An organization should consider all the risks it faces, from whatever source.

The risk identification process should be carried out systematically, rather than in an ad hoc fashion. A systematic approach should ensure that all aspects of risk are properly considered, and that nothing of significance is overlooked. The responsibilities for identifying risks should be clearly assigned to particular individuals or departments. If an organization has a risk manager, this individual might be given the overall responsibility for coordinating the risk identification process. The identification of risks should, however, consider all the risks facing the organization, not just particular types of risk such as financial risks only.

Organizations face a very large number of risks, such that a single individual or group of individuals might be unable to identify all of them. The risk environment is also too complex and dynamic for just a small number of individuals to appreciate it fully. Risk identification will therefore benefit from discussions and consultations with managers and employees who are in a good position to understand the risks that arise in their area of the business and offer their views as to what should be done to deal with them or exploit them.

The process might start with the board of directors initiating a periodic risk review. The board might discuss risks facing the business, and are likely to commission reports from management to obtain in-depth analysis and opinions. Selected employees might be encouraged to contribute to the process, by meeting regularly to discuss risks, how they are being dealt with and what the potential hazards (or opportunities) might be.

The risk identification process should be *timely*, in the sense that risks should be identified in time either to avoid unnecessary losses or to take advantage of available opportunities while they still exist.

- There is little value in recognizing an opportunity when it is too late to do anything about it.

- If a threat is recognized at a late stage, the measures needed to deal with it might have to be more drastic, and the losses incurred might be greater than if the threat had been spotted and dealt with earlier.

Risk identification should also be a *continual process*, rather than an ocasional one-off exercise. The risk environment changes, with some risks becoming more significant and others less so over time. New risks also arise. By carrying out regular risk assessments, it should be possible to monitor changes that have occurred and take a view on whether a different strategy or new control or containment measures are now required.

There are two elements of thinking in risk identification.

- One approach is to address the problem of risk from the perspective of earnings growth, and identify the risks that could prevent the organization from achieving its earnings growth targets. This approach is used for analysing two-way risks, for example, and business planning.

- A second approach, based more on risk insurance management, is to consider the worst events that might happen as an essential first step towards developing contingency plans, such as disaster recovery plans, or arranging suitable insurance cover.

Risk scanning and environmental mapping

Risk identification starts with a scanning process, based on the classifications of risk that it uses. For each risk environment or risk classification, there are potential risks (both downside risks and two-way risks). Risks vary for each organization, because organizations operate in differing risk environments, and the following examples of risk scanning are illustrative only.

- In the social environment, a risk might be identified in the changing age distribution of a country's population. In a country where average life expectancy is lengthening and the birth rate is slowing, a large proportion of the population will eventually be over normal retirement age. For some organizations, this could give rise to either a threat or an opportunity.

- In the legal and regulatory environment, risks can arise from new legislation and measures might be necessary to comply with the new regulations. For example, with the implementation of elements of the Financial Services and Markets Act in the UK in 2001, firms of solicitors and accountants involved in financial services work had to assess the implications for their business and how to avoid criminal liability for a breach of the Act. Legal change can create opportunities as well as threats: for example, any proposal to de-criminalize an activity, such as the sale of cannabis, would give rise to new opportunities for legitimate businesses.

- In the operating environment, there are both business risks and financial risks. Organizations might identify risks in the volatility of prices in the financial markets, a lack of suitably trained employees, new technological developments and low investment in research and development, or a lack of successful new products.

Environmental mapping is a process of identifying the threats and opportunities that face the organization as a consequence of the environmental risks. Many of these threats and opportunities are likely to relate to risks in the operating environment. The list below is again illustrative only, and is not intended to show threats or opportunities facing all organizations.

- IT systems are vulnerable to attacks from hackers and viruses. The risk for a company might be that a hacker will successfully gain access to a system and either copy, delete or alter the information contained in it.

- Manufacturing processes and systems might be vulnerable to excessive costs. The risk might be that unless the company changes its systems, it will be unable to compete globally with its competitors. On the other hand, the introduction of new manufacturing processes such as work cell organization and just-in-time manufacturing might give the company an opportunity to reduce production costs and compete more effectively.

- An organization might be vulnerable to a shortage of skilled staff. The risk might be that unless new staff can be recruited and trained, plans for expansion and development of the business might have to be deferred.

- Some companies might need to be aware of the threat from international pressure groups and the risk to their reputation in the eyes of the general public. A number of companies have been significantly affected in recent times by reputational issues, relating to concerns such as oil and gas exploration, experimentation on live animals, genetically-modified crops and the price of drugs and medicines to Third World countries.

- There are risks in business strategy. In a competitive market, a company has to be alert to what the competition is doing. The environmental risk could be that a competitor introducing a successful new product might take a large share of the market. The company would be particularly vulnerable if it is unable to respond to the competitive threat quickly due to underinvestment in research and development.

To identify operational risks, a link has to be made between the nature of risks in the environment and why these could have an impact on the organization. This calls for a good understanding of the products and services of the business and the marketplace in which it operates. Using this understanding and knowledge, consideration should be given to risks in the business process, to the quality of the local management team and to how people might behave in different situations. In addition, thought should be given to the potential effect on operations of changes in the external risk environment.

The risks that are identified should not be too general, because it will not be possible to devise a strategy for managing them. Risks should be specific to company or to the industry sector in which it operates. It will be useful to relate risks to the critical success factors (CSFs) for the company. A significant risk is one that would create an obstacle to any of the CSFs.

At the end of the environmental mapping process, an organization should have identified a number of threats and opportunities facing the business as a consequence of various environmental risks.

Exposures to risk

A risk in the environment affects an organization only if it has an exposure to it. Without exposure, there is no risk, and the greater the exposure, the greater the risk. Exposures can be categorized in different ways.

Financial exposures can be stated in money terms. For example, credit risk exposure can be expressed in terms of the amount of outstanding debts that the organization is owed by its customers. Foreign exchange risk exposure can be expressed as the net difference between assets and liabilities of an organization in a particular currency. For example, if a UK company has a balance of €3 million in its euros account but owes its suppliers €5 million, it has a currency exposure of net liabilities of €2 million.

Physical asset exposures are probably most easily associated with insurable risks, such as the risk of damage through accident or vandalism, or loss through theft. Exposures can be expressed in terms of the number of assets of a particular type, such as the number of properties or their floor area, an amount of inventory, a quantity of motor vehicles, a number of computers and terminals, and so on. Exposures could also be expressed in terms of revenue or expenditure, such as the loss of income or increase in costs that would occur if a particular asset were to be damaged or lost.

Human asset exposures can be expressed in terms of numbers of employees or managers. Risks can arise out of contractual or other legal obligations towards employees, accident and health risks and productivity issues. The education and training of employees can be seen as an opportunity to benefit from improved skills and productivity, with 'up-side' risk potential.

Some exposures might be expressed in terms of *liabilities*, such as legal liabilities or liabilities arising from environmental damage or pollution.

Risk identification overload

If too many risks are identified, it becomes very difficult to identify and manage those that are significant. Too much effort might be spent on risks that are not serious and for which control or containment measures generate only small benefits. Management should focus its efforts on significant risks, which can be defined as those that are potentially damaging to the achievement of corporate objectives.

To avoid risk identification overload, the total number of identified risks should therefore be reduced to a manageable number of significant risks. Perhaps 20 – 30 significant risks is a realistic total, although the circumstances will vary between different companies.

It might be useful to look at what senior management in top UK companies have seen as the major strategic risks facing their companies. In 1999, Deloitte and Touche published a survey of listed companies into what they considered to be the most significant risks facing them. Respondents were asked to grade risks on a scale of 1 (low risk) to 9 (very high risk). The top perceived risks were as follows.

	Average rating score
Failure to manage major projects	7.05
Failure of strategy	6.67
Failure to innovate	6.32
Poor reputation/brand management	6.30
Lack of employee motivation and poor performance	6.00

2.4   Techniques for identifying risks and exposures

Risk identification and measurement techniques range from the elementary (discussions of risk) to the complex.

The banking industry has developed advanced techniques for identifying risks and measuring exposures, and many banks have sophisticated computerized risk-assessment models. The products and services offered by banks are priced to allow for the perceived risk. For example, the interest rate charged on a loan reflects the perceived credit risk of the customer as well as the general level of interest rates. Banks have also developed computer models to evaluate operational risks as well as credit risks in their lending operations and financial risks in their trading operations.

For many companies, risk assessment is much less sophisticated, and they might use a variety of techniques to identify risks and exposures. Whatever techniques are used, the overall responsibility for risk management rests with the board of directors although responsibilities for risk identification should be delegated and clearly assigned to particular individual managers.

Environmental mapping techniques, described above, might be used by a working party set up to identify risks. For example, a company might arrange a regular meeting of senior executives to discuss risk and consider risk management strategies, with environmental mapping used as the starting point for the discussions.

Since risk identification procedures should be carried out regularly and systematically, *checklists* might be used. Checklists have the advantage of providing guidelines to management about what aspects of the risk environment to consider, and how these might affect the organization. However, checklists also have their disadvantages.

- If a checklist is prepared in-house by the organization's own staff, it might be flawed, omitting aspects of risk that ought to be considered. In-house managers might be unable to think broadly enough, outside their direct experiences.

- If a checklist is somehow obtained from an external source, it will not be fully applicable to the particular circumstances of the organization. The risk environment is also dynamic, which means that unless a checklist is regularly amended to allow for changing risks, it could become out-of-date and unsuitable for use.

Some risks might be identified from *financial information*. Investors use the published annual report and financial statements of companies to assess their performance and financial position. Managers have access to more detailed financial information and special reports, and can use this to identify risks. In particular, they can analyse budgets and forecasts of profitability and cash flows, and the assumptions on which these are based, to assess the vulnerability of the company to variations in actual outcomes.

Other risks might be identified from *legal documentation*, such as contracts with suppliers, customers or employees. Statutes and regulations might be read to establish what the consequences of non-compliance might be.

Insights into risk from individuals directly involved in operations can be extremely valuable. Risk managers might therefore *interview* managers and employees to obtain their views about risk, and then produce a summary of opinions.

For certain types of risk, such as health and safety risk, pollution risk, fire risk and so on, *site visits* should provide useful information for identifying significant risks. Regular site visits should be an element of the embedded risk management system, and will give risk managers a better understanding.

Some risks might be identified retrospectively from a *statistical analysis of historical records*. Insurance companies use historical information in deciding the premium to charge on an insurance policy. In the same way, a company can use historical records to identify losses that have arisen in the past and identify their likely cause. The following examples might be useful illustrations.

A company might identify from historical records a direct correlation between the volume of sales and the weather. Impulse purchases of ice cream, for example, might vary with the temperature. In such cases, the company would identify weather conditions as a source of risk.

A company might learn from an analysis of e-mails that employees are spending large amounts of their time each day dealing with unnecessary e-mail messages. If so, the IT environment would be a risk to productivity.

An organization might use *outside consultants* to assist with risk identification. The main advantage of using consultants should be to gain the benefit of their expertise and experience, and also their independent judgement. However, risk identification should be a part of an ongoing risk management system, and at some stage the use of consultants should give way to other techniques and methods.

A tendency with risk identification might be to focus on what has happened in the past. Past losses should certainly provide a guide to the risk of future losses. However, as the risk environment changes, the likelihood of losses from different sources will also change, and new opportunities to benefit from changing circumstances will arise. Risk assessment should therefore include a forward-looking element, to identify new risks that could arise and their implications for the organization.

A checklist approach to risk identification

With a checklist approach to identifying risks, the starting point might be a list of potential risks. By working through the list, management might identify risks that apply to their own organization. The problem with this approach, as indicated above, is that a list prepared externally cannot allow for differences between organizations, or unique circumstances.

An illustrative checklist is shown below. It is based on a checklist provided in the Boardroom Briefing to the Turnbull Report. (The Turnbull Report, which was written in 1999 as part of the development of corporate governance in the UK, is described in a later chapter. Its focus is on internal controls and risk-based management in top UK companies. The Boardroom Briefing on the Report was produced by a working party chaired by Nigel Turnbull, after whom the report is named.) The checklist focuses primarily on down-side risks, but you might find the list useful as an indication of the wide range of potential risks that might face companies. See how many you can relate to the organization where you work. Remember that the list is in no way comprehensive.

Business risk or strategic risk

Selecting the wrong business strategy.

Changing conditions in the regional, national or world economy having an effect on the company's business.

Political risk, for example political instability in a particular geographical market, or country where key raw materials are obtained.

The risk from the consequences of a new or ongoing government policy.

Technological change: the risk of obsolescent technology or the impact of new technology.

Competition, and its threat to prices. The risk of losing market share to rival firms.

Threats to the company's markets from substitute products.

Becoming a takeover target.

Making a poor acquisition.

Being unable to raise new capital for investment.

Being too slow to innovate.

Being in an industry in decline.

Financial risks

A shortage of cash (liquidity risk).

Risks from adverse movements in market prices, such as the company's own share price (market risk).

The risk of insolvency and inability to remain in business as a going concern.

A risk of trying to expand the business too quickly with too little capital ('overtrading' risk).

The risk of customer bad debts (credit risk) or non-paying borrowers.

The risk of adverse movement in interest rates (interest-rate risk).

The risk to profits and cash flows from adverse movements in foreign exchange rates (currency risk).

A risk of losses due to fraud.

A breakdown in the company's accounting system.

Having unreliable accounting records.

Having liabilities that are unrecorded. For example, a company might have given guarantees about which senior management is unaware.

Taking decisions with incomplete or inaccurate financial information.

Making promises to shareholders that cannot be fulfilled.

Compliance risks

These are risks from a failure to comply with the law and regulations.

Breaching financial regulations.

Breaching the requirements of the Companies Act.

Litigation risk.

Breaching competition laws.

Incurring tax penalties.

Breaching the regulations on value added tax.

Health and safety risks.

Environmental issues (eg aspects of operations that have implications for pollution of the land, the air or water sources, or the destruction of the earth's natural resources.)

Operational and other risks

The commercial failure of a new product or service. Businesses usually need to have a continual stream of new products coming to the market, to take the place of existing products nearing the end of their commercial life.

A failure to satisfy customers.

A failure to provide a sufficient level of service. For example, a railway company might fail to provide a sufficient number of train journeys, or to run a sufficient number of their services on time.

Quality problems, and the threat to sales and profits from poor-quality products or services.

The loss of a key contract.

An over-reliance on one or two key suppliers or customers. The risk is that a customer might takes his business elsewhere, or a supplier might go out of business.

A lack of orders from customers.

Missed business opportunities.

A lack of employee motivation resulting in poor efficiency or ineffective work practices.

The failure of a large technology-related project. Investment in high-technology and new-technology projects is invariably very risky.

Problems with succession at the top of the company. For example, the chief executive might be nearing retirement age, without any successor having been identified and groomed to replace him.

A loss of key people.

A shortage of labour skills.

A stock-out of key raw materials.

A failure to reduce the company's operating cost base, so that operating costs are too high, threatening the ability of the company to remain competitive.

A loss of physical fixed assets, for example through fire, accident or theft.

A loss of intangible fixed assets, such as intellectual property.

Failure to exploit intellectual property that the company owns, such as patent rights, trademark rights, or copyrights. Poor brand management.

Failure of a supplier of out-sourced services, such as vehicle fleet maintenance or facilities management, to provide a proper service.

A failure to align business processes with the strategic goals of the company.

A loss of entrepreneurial spirit.

A physical disaster, such as a fire or flooding.

Vulnerability of IT systems to unauthorized access by hackers or attacks by viruses.

Business probity problems affecting the reputational risk of the company. If a company (or any employee) is suspected of dishonest or dubious business practices, its loss of reputation could deter customers from doing business with it.

Other problems with the company's reputation in the eyes of its customers, or the public in general.

2.5   From identifying risks to risk analysis

Risks can be identified using a variety of different techniques, but the process calls for a combination of judgement, experience and analysis. The next stage in the risk management process is the quantification or measurement of risks, to establish their significance, often using statistical techniques.

Risk analysis is the subject of the next chapter.

Responsibility for risk management in the corporate

Introducing a risk-based approach to management requires the full support of operational managers, but in the UK, the ultimate responsibility for risk management in listed companies (and by implication, other companies too) belongs with the board of directors. This responsibility is made clear in the Combined Code for UK listed companies, reinforced by the Turnbull Report, which are described more fully in a later chapter.

A task for the board is to decide how best to establish and operate a risk management system. To apply a risk-based approach to management, the following continual cycle of events should be established.

- The board of directors should identify key internal and external changes that have occurred, and reconsider and agree clear objectives for the company.

- The board should also *identify the Critical Success Factors* (CSFs) for the company. These are the factors that are critical to the achievement of those objectives. Unless performance in respect of each CSF is satisfactory, the objectives of the company will be unattainable.

- Risks facing the company should be *identified and prioritized*. The prioritization of risks is part of the risk analysis process.

- The number of risks on the list is likely to be very large, and there will be insufficient management time to deal with all of them. The list should be reduced to just those risks that are significant. A typical listed company might have about 20 to 25 significant risks.

- Management should *formulate strategies for controlling and containing the risks*. The board of directors should then agree the risk control strategies and risk management policy.

- *Responsibility and accountability* for risk management at an operational level should be agreed with the individuals concerned.

- There should be broad and regular *consultation with employees* about risks, to create greater risk awareness.

- *Changes in culture* and behaviour should be encouraged, and managers and other employees should acquire the habit of focusing on the fundamentals of good risk management and internal control.

- *Early warning mechanisms* should be put in place, both to identify potential 'trouble' as soon as it is detectable, and also to identify new opportunities to exploit.

- The significant elements of *internal control* should be monitored.

- The board of directors should seek sources of assurance that the system of risk management and internal control is functioning as intended and that the system is effective. There are two issues here. First, the system that the board has put in place has to be operated properly. Secondly, the system, operating properly, should achieve the purposes for which it was designed.

- There should be *regular reporting by management to the board* on risk issues, and an assessment of risk should feature in decision-making.

- The board of directors should *review* risk and internal control regularly, prior to end-of-year reporting to shareholders.

- Where appropriate, steps should be taken to improve the system. The risk management system should evolve and change continually, in response to changes in circumstances.

Identifying risks: top-down or bottom-up approach

Information for the identification of risks originates both inside and outside the organization, and successful risk identification depends on having access to various information sources. The approach to identifying risks could be top-down, bottom-up or a combination of the two.

In a top-down approach, the risk identification process starts with the board of directors, who might have a series of brainstorming meetings, calling in key executive managers to help them. The board might then communicate its views to senior management, and ask for their considered views.

In a bottom-up approach, a number of local focus groups or working parties are set up, each under the supervision of a manager with risk-management experience. Each group discusses risks and reaches a view on the risks that seem most significant for its particular area of the business. The views of all the focus groups are then consolidated into a single report to the board of directors.

Implementing the system

Although the board of directors has the ultimate responsibility for risk management, the task of putting a risk-management system into operation depends on executive management. Individual managers should be given responsibility for risk, and held accountable to the board. A major threat to the successful implementation of a risk-management system is the inability of a board of directors to win the support of its executive management team.

Some companies employ a risk manager, or even a risk-management team. Other companies have an internal audit department that might carry out investigations into aspects of risk and risk management. Risk managers and internal auditors should not have the responsibility for risk management, although they should be responsible for checking that the system of risk management is operating as intended. They should assist and advise line managers, but should not be in a position to instruct them.

3

RISK ANALYSIS

After reading this chapter, you should:

● Understand various ways in which risk might be analysed

● Understand the role of statistics in risk analysis

● Be aware of several techniques of measuring risk.

3.1   Measuring risk statistically

The previous chapter looked at the different types of risk that might face an organization. The next step in a risk-based approach to management is to apply a method for assessing the size and significance of individual risks, in order to identify the most serious and to consider methods of controlling or containing them.

We often assume that individuals can evaluate risk logically, but in practice they often do not. For example, many people in the UK do not realize that if they buy a National Lottery ticket one hour before the draw, the risk of dying before the draw is greater than the chance of winning the jackpot. Mathematical analysis of risk allows managers to avoid any misconceptions or misunderstanding about their significance.

The most appropriate method of measuring risk mathematically will depend on the nature of the risk. Different types of risk can be measured in different ways.

Probability analysis as a method of measuring risk

We talk in general terms of 'the risk of fraud' and 'the risk of an accident', and we might use the word descriptively, such as saying that a particular course of action 'carries a lot of (downside) risk'. Downside risk can often be measured in terms of probabilities, such as there is a 50% chance of making a loss, provided that information exists to make a reliable probability estimate.

However, an outcome could have an upside potential as well as downside risk. In these circumstances, risk could be measured in terms of the range of outcomes that are possible, from the most upside to the most downside. For example, if we look at two investments, X and Y, the range of possible returns for X might be 6% - 10%, and for Y it might be 2% - 14%. If so, Y would probably be considered more risky, because a crude mathematical measure of risk is simply the range of possible outcomes. Y seems more risky because the range of outcomes is broader, and the worst possible outcome for Y is worse than for X.

However, a simple range of possible outcomes is not a satisfactory measure of risk because the probability of each outcome might differ. In the case of investments X and Y, investment Y might be more likely to have a return near the higher end of the potential range, whereas investment X might be more likely to have a return at the lower end of the expected range. If so, Y would offer the higher expected return, but a comparison of the ranges of possible outcomes for each investment would not necessarily on its own indicate which investment had the higher risk element.

A technique for comparing investments or alternative courses of action might therefore be on the basis of both their *expected return* and their *expected risk*, with risk measured as the possible variations in the actual outcome around their expected value.

- An expected return is an average return you would expect to get if you repeated an activity many times over. It is the weighted average value of probable outcomes. For example, if an investment has a 50% chance of making a profit of £10,000 and a 50% chance of making a loss of £2000, the expected return (ie the expected value of the return) would be a profit of £4,000. For one-off or occasional events, a knowledge of the expected return might not be much help in deciding what to do and whether to take on a risk. In the example above, if a one-off investment has an equal chance of making either a profit of £10,000 or a loss of £2,000, it does not necessarily help to know that the expected value of profit is £4,000.

- Risk can be measured as a statistical variation around the expected value. The possibility of a range of outcomes for regularly-repeated events leads to the idea of the bell-shaped curve, a normal distribution of probabilities and statistical analysis using the standard deviation of the expected return.

The concept of *utility* might also be taken into account in risk analysis. The utility of a loss to you might be greater than the utility of an equal gain. In other words you might be much more upset about losing £2,000 than pleased by gaining £10,000. Given an investment with an equal probability of an outcome of plus £10,000 or minus £2,000, some individuals would play for safety and decide against making the investment.

Utility might be also be important with respect to risks where an adverse outcome could have very damaging effects, such as reputational risk. For a well-established company, the risk from an adverse event might be sufficient to make it prefer to avoid any exposure to a risk of reputational damage. A notable example was the adverse effect on the reputation of auditors Andersen of the collapse of its audit client Enron in 2001, and the very bad publicity for Andersen that followed.

Yet another technique of risk analysis is the idea of reversion to the mean. Suppose that a company operating a ski centre is aware that the success of its business varies to some extent with the atmospheric temperature. Historical data shows that the on average the midday temperature in February at its centre is minus 10 degrees, but that over the past four years or so, the average temperature has been minus 5 degrees. The technique of reversion to the mean would suggest that over the long term the average February temperature will remain minus five degrees. This suggests that there is every chance of lower temperatures in February next year. This technique is only valid, however, if the historical analysis of a trend is reliable, and the underlying situation remains the same so that the same trend can be expected to continue. A change in circumstances, such as general global warming, could break the historical statistical relationship between temperature and time of year.

3.2 The size of an exposure to risk and the amount at risk

Risk exists only when there is exposure, and increases with the size of the exposure. An exposure can often be measured as a total amount of money whose value would be affected by a worse-than or more-favourable-than outcome than expected.

However, the amount of money at risk is usually not the full amount of the exposure. For example, a UK company holding $150,000 has an exposure to a fall in the value of the dollar against sterling. If the dollar were to fall in value against sterling from, say, £1 = $1.25 to £1 = $1.50, the sterling value of the company's dollars would fall from £120,000 to £100,000 and the loss would be £20,000. For the company to lose the full value of its original exposure, dollars would have to lose all their value.

Similarly, with an exposure to credit risk, the potential loss is not usually the full amount of the exposure. If a bank has lent £50,000 to a company, the borrower might become insolvent and be unable to repay the loan. Conceivably, the bank would lose the full £50,000. More likely is the probability that the bank would recover some of the money when the business of the borrower is liquidated.

The same principle applies to exposures that are measurable as physical assets or human assets. A company might own a building valued at £10 million, and has an exposure to damage from fire. In an event of fire, however, the size of the potential loss from building damage will not be as much as £10 million. Similarly, if a company employs 100 people at a production plant, it will have an exposure to the risk of an accident at work. Potentially, exposure all 100 of the staff could be injured in an accident at work, but this outcome would be highly improbable.

The *size* of a risk depends not so much on the size of the exposure, but rather on the potential loss (or gain) in the event that an unexpected outcome occurs.

The potential loss or gain from a risk exposure

The measurement of the potential loss or gain differs according to whether the risk is pure or speculative. With pure risk (downside risk) an exposure creates a potential for an unexpected loss. With exposure to speculative risk, there is the possibility of either an unexpected loss or an unexpected gain.

With **pure risk**, there are two dimensions to the exposure to loss:

● the **frequency** of adverse outcomes, or the **probability** that an adverse outcome will occur, and

● the **severity** or **impact** of the loss when an adverse outcome does occur.

The risk of loss is obviously significant when adverse outcomes are frequent and the severity of the loss on each occasion is high, and relatively insignificant when an adverse outcome is infrequent and the impact of any loss is low.

With **speculative risk**, there are also two dimensions to potential for loss or gain:

● the **frequency** of both positive and negative outcomes, and

● the **range of possible outcomes**, both positive and negative, around the expected outcome.

The size of any unexpected gain or loss will clearly be greater when outcomes above or below expectation are frequent, and there are wide variations in possible outcomes. (The range of possible outcomes is often dependent on the **volatility** of one or more factors. For example, an exposure to foreign exchange risk is usually a speculative risk, and the size of the risk depends on the volatility of the exchange rate.)

3.3   Risk profiling (risk mapping)

A technique for profiling pure risk as a step towards analysing risks and prioritizing them is to 'map' the risks in a matrix. The purpose of risk profiling is to identify those risks that seem to be the most significant (the greatest), so that priority attention can be given to them.

The two sides of the matrix represent the frequency of adverse outcomes and the severity of the loss when an adverse outcome occurs. It is a single-period model, and the frequency or probability of an adverse outcome relates to the likelihood that it will occur during the planning period.

		Severity/impact	
		Low	**High**
Frequency/ probability	**Low**	Low probability, low impact	High probability, low impact
	High	Low probability, high impact	High probability, high impact

Risks in the bottom right hand corner of the matrix are more significant than other risks, and risks in the top left hand corner are the least significant. Risks in the top right hand corner or bottom left hand corner lie somewhere in the middle.

The value of risk profiling as a method of risk measurement is that by categorizing risks, management can make an initial judgement about which risks are more significant than others. A conceptual approach to prioritizing risks based on this two-by-two matrix of risk impact and probability of occurrence might be as follows.

Impact	Probability	Action
High	High	Take immediate action to deal with the risk.
High	Low	Consider action. Have a contingency plan in the event of an adverse outcome.
Low	High	Consider action to deal with the risk
Low	Low	Keep the risk under periodic review, as part of the regular risk-assessment process.

Risks with a low likelihood of happening but a high impact are often suitable for containment through *insurance*.

The risk-measurement matrix is sometimes drawn as a three-by-three matrix, as follows.

		Severity/impact		
		Low		**High**
	Low	1	2	3
Frequency/ probability		4	5	6
	High	7	8	9

This matrix allows for more gradings in the prioritization of risks. The most significant risks will be those mapped in boxes 9, 6 and 8 of the matrix, and the least significant are those in boxes 1, 2 and 4. Risks that lie somewhere in the middle are those falling in boxes 3, 5 and 7.

Another non-statistical approach to analysing the frequency or probability of an adverse outcome is to use four measurements:

● Almost nil. In the opinion of the person analysing the risk, an adverse outcome will not happen.

● Slight. An adverse outcome has not happened yet, and is unlikely to happen. Nevertheless, it is a possibility.

● Moderate. An adverse outcome has occurred from time to time in the past, and will probably happen again at some time in the future.

● Definite. An adverse outcome has occurred frequently in the past and will continue to occur regularly in the future.

3.4 Measuring pure risk: expected value of loss

For exposures to both pure risk and speculative risk, management might wish to measure the potential loss or gain in money terms. For each risk, it is desirable to know:

● the expected value of the loss or gain in the planning period, and

● possible variations in outcome from one planning period to the next.

Pure risk can be measured as an expected value of loss in the budget period, as the product of the probability of an adverse outcome in the period and an average amount of loss incurred in the event of such an outcome. An expected value (EV) is simply a weighted average value, based on probabilities

Probability x Average loss severity = Expected value of loss

For example, a company operating in one building might estimate that the probability of fire during the year is 5% and that if a fire occurs, the damage would be between £10,000 and £500,000, but on average would be £250,000. The expected value of loss from fire damage during any year would therefore be 5% x £250,000 = £12,500. The company's risk manager might compare this expected value of loss with the cost of the premium for fire risk insurance.

Example: estimating the expected loss on loans

A bank might estimate its risk from credit default in a similar way. Suppose that a bank has a loan book of £100 million in secured loans, and from an analysis of historical records, it estimates that 4% of borrowers will default during the year. It also estimates that in an event of default, the bank will recover 80% of the loans from their security. The expected value of loss from the credit risk in the loan book would therefore be £100 million x 4% x 20% = £800,000.

The estimated future recovery value of a loan, in an event of default by the borrower, depends on factors such as:

● The relative bargaining position of lender and borrower

● The underlying bankruptcy code and its enforceability. It is particularly important to distinguish the codes applying to sovereign and corporate borrowers.

● Access to collateral in the event of default. This is linked to the rules of the national bankruptcy code.

● The seniority of the loan or bond, and whether it is secured or not.

● The availability of secured collateral, and its value in conditions of distress.

● Multiple creditors and the existence or absence of bank debt.

Past experience can be used to produce a mathematical assessment of the probable recovery value in each particular case.

(Contractual and organizational provisions can be made to limit the credit risk. For example, contractual provisions might provide for netting, so that if you owe organization X £1 million and the organization X owes you £1.8 million, the debts are netted so that organization X owes you just £800,000. This is important in the event of insolvency. If organization X becomes insolvent, you will have just £800,000 at risk. Without netting, you would be obliged to pay the £1 million you owe, and you would have a debt of £1.8 million from organization X at risk.

Organizational provisions might include credit committees of senior managers to decide which organizations can be used as counterparties for financial transactions such as interest-rate swaps.)

3.5 Maximum possible outcome and maximum probable outcome

An expected value of loss is a single-figure measurement, representing an average loss in any planning period. The actual loss in any planning period could be higher or lower than the average. Management should wish to know just how large the loss might be if it does occur. This can be stated as either a maximum possible outcome or a maximum probable outcome. The maximum possible outcome is the most that the loss could possibly be, whereas the maximum probable outcome is the largest loss that management thinks might occur.

For example, a bank with a loan book of £100 million of unsecured loans estimates that 4% of borrowers will default during the year, and that only 25% of these loans will be recovered. The expected value of the loss would therefore be £100 million x 4% x 75% = £3 million. The maximum possible loss would be £100 million. Management might judge, however, that defaults are most unlikely to exceed 15% and that at least 10% of loans will be recovered in an event of default. The maximum probable loss would therefore be £100 million x 15% x 90% = £13.5 million.

Information about both the expected value of loss and the maximum probable loss should help management to reach a decision on how the risk should be controlled.

When the maximum probable loss is be significantly larger than the expected value of the loss, management will have to consider what is the most appropriate method of containing the risk. Fire risk provides a useful example. Suppose that a company with ten similar buildings estimates that the probability of a fire at any building during the year is 4%, and that the average expected loss from fire damage would be £50,000. The expected value of loss from fire damage in the year would therefore be 10 buildings x 4% x £50,000 = £20,000. If an insurance company offers fire insurance cover on all the buildings for an annual premium of, say, £40,000, the company might consider taking on the fire risk itself and not bothering with insurance. However, suppose that management believes it possible that two buildings might suffer fire damage in the year, and the loss could be up to £100,000 at each building. The maximum probable loss would be (2 x £100,000) £200,000. In view of this, management might decide that it would be prudent to take out insurance for £40,000 rather than be exposed to a risk of losses of up to £200,000.

3.6 Probability distributions and pure risk analysis

Probability distributions can be used to analyse risk. A probability distribution shows what the possible outcomes of an event might be, and the probability of each of those outcomes. The total value of a probability distribution must be 100% (or 1.0), representing all possible outcomes.

Suppose that a manufacturing company is measuring the risk of losses from leakages in an oil pipe. It estimates that there could be between 0 and 4 leakages next year, and that the probabilities are as follows.

Number of incidents	Probability
0	0.25
1	0.35
2	0.15
3	0.10
4	0.05
Total	1.00

The weighted average number of incidents (ie the expected value of the number of incidents) is calculated as the total of each possible outcome multiplied by its associated probability.

Number of incidents (n)	Probability (p)	Expected value (sum of np)
0	0.25	0.00
1	0.35	0.35
2	0.15	0.30
3	0.10	0.30
4	0.05	0.20
Total	1.00	1.15

In this example, the expected number of incidents in the year will be 1.15, but this is an average of the probability distribution of possible outcomes. The expected value can be used to measure an average expected loss, whereas the probability distribution could be used to analyse the range of what might happen. Here, for example, management can estimate that there is a 95% probability that the total number of leakages will not exceed three during the year. This is the sum of the probabilities of an outcome of 0, 1, 2 or 3 leakages.

When a probability distribution exists for more than one uncertain outcome, a distribution of *joint probabilities* can be derived. A joint probability is the probability that two things will occur together. For example, suppose that there is a 20% probability that employee A and a 30% probability that employee B will each be absent from work on at least 5 days each year. If absences from work by each of the employees are in no way related to each other, the joint probability that both employees will be absent for at least five days in the next year is calculated by multiplying the probability of each individual outcome. In this example, it would be 20% x 30%, or 6% (0.20 x 0.30 = 0.06).

A probability distribution of joint probabilities can be drawn up. Suppose for example that a bank with a loan book of £100 million has made the following estimates of defaults by borrowers and the loss in the event of a default. (The loss is the amount owed by the borrower less the recovery value of the loan.)

Default rate	Probability	Loss in event of default	Probability
4%	0.30	20%	0.20
5%	0.50	25%	0.60
6%	0.20	30%	0.20
	1.00		1.00

The actual loss will be the default rate multiplied by the loss in the event of default. The expected value of the default rate is (0.30 x 4% + 0.50 x 5% + 0.20 x 6%) 4.9%, and the expected value of the loss on default will be 25% (workings not shown). The expected value of losses in the year from default will therefore be £100 million x 4.9% x 25% = £1.225 million. A joint probability distribution can be calculated to show what the possible variation in the losses might be.

Default rate	Probability	Loss in event of default	Probability	Joint probability	Loss for this outcome
					£m
4%	0.30	20%	0.20	0.06	0.80
4%	0.30	25%	0.60	0.18	1.00
4%	0.30	30%	0.20	0.06	1.20
5%	0.50	20%	0.20	0.10	1.00
5%	0.50	25%	0.60	0.30	1.25
5%	0.50	30%	0.20	0.10	1.50
6%	0.20	20%	0.20	0.04	1.20
6%	0.20	25%	0.60	0.12	1.50
6%	0.20	30%	0.20	<u>0.04</u>	1.80
				<u>1.00</u>	

The loss for each outcome is the size of the loan book multiplied by both the probability of default and the loss in the event of default.

The joint probability distribution gives management measurements of the default risk that supplement the weighted average expected value. For example, there is a probability of (0.10 + 0.12 + 0.04) 0.26 or 26% that the loss will be £1.5 million or more.

Standard deviation as a measure of variation

Standard deviation is another statistical measure of the possible variations of actual outcomes around the expected or average outcome. It is a form of average variation. The formula for calculating the standard deviation for items in a sample is:

$$\sqrt{\frac{\Sigma\, f(x-\bar{x})^2}{n}}$$

Where:

x is the value of each possible outcome

$\bar{x}$ is the expected value (average) of all the possible outcomes

f is the frequency of the outcome

Σ means 'sum of'

n is the number of items in the sample.

Suppose that a company is estimating the loss of output due to absenteeism from work, and wishes to obtain a measure of the number of man-days lost each week due to unscheduled absences from work. Records for the past 50 weeks might show the days lost to be as follows.

Man-days lost per week	Number of occasions	
x	f	fx
20	7	140
25	12	300
30	14	420
35	10	350
40	5	200
45	2	90
	50	1,500

The average number of man-days lost each week was (1,500/50) 30. The standard deviation of man-days lost is calculated as follows.

Man-days lost per week	Number of occasions		
x	f	$x - \bar{x}$	$f(x-\bar{x})^2$
20	7	-10	700
25	12	-5	300
30	14	0	0
35	10	5	250
40	5	10	500
45	2	15	450
	50		2,200

The standard deviation is $\dfrac{2200}{50} = 6.63$ days.

The statistical significance of the standard deviation is not explained here. However, it is a weighted measure of variations in outcome around the average value, and a higher standard deviation relative to the expected value indicates a wider range of possible outcomes. If certain assumptions are made about the probability distribution of possible outcomes, measures of standard deviation can be used to provide a statistical analysis of probabilities.

3.7 Statistical measurement of speculative (two-way) risk

Statistical analysis can also be used to measure speculative risk (two-way risk). To measure speculative risk mathematically, management needs an estimate of variations above and below the expected outcome. These can be estimated as a standard deviation in the value of outcomes around the expected average. For example, it might be estimated that the average sterling/US dollar exchange rate next year will be £1 = $1.40, but the standard deviation in this estimate might be, say, 8 cents.

Measurement of subjective risk also calls for an estimate of **volatility**. Volatility refers not just to the size of movements in a particular value, but also the frequency of the movements. Suppose that the sterling/US dollar exchange rate is measured daily over two six-day periods, as follows.

Period 1 Day	Exchange rate	Change	Period 2 Day	Exchange rate	Change
1	$1.43		1	$1.375	
2	$1.36	- 0.07	2	$1.385	+ 0.01
3	$1.39	+ 0.03	3	$1.395	+ 0.01
4	$1.43	+ 0.04	4	$1.405	+ 0.01
5	$1.37	- 0.06	5	$1.415	+ 0.01
6	$1.42	+ 0.05	6	$1.425	+ 0.01

The average exchange rate over each six-day period is $1.40. The range within which the exchange rate moves is also roughly the same in each period, between $1.36 and $1.43 in period 1 and $1.375 and $1.425 in period 2. However, the volatility is much greater in period 1, because the size of the changes in the rate, up and down, is much more varied than in period 2, where the change was a constant $0.01 each day. In fact, in period 2, there is no volatility at all, because the daily price movement is constant.

Volatility creates risk, and potential for either unexpected gains or losses. Examples of volatility are found in the financial markets, where there are continual changes in exchange rates, equity share prices and interest rates. Prices in the financial markets can move up or down substantially, and in addition, daily price movements up or down can also be large and unpredictable. Not surprisingly, price volatility is a major risk for banks, which trade extensively in currency, interest-rate and equity instruments.

3.8   Simulation models

Some aspects of risk can be analysed and measured by a simulation model, which is a model representation of the 'real world'. In some instances, it might be a physical model or a model constructed with computer graphics. In aircraft manufacturing, for example, safety is tested with wind tunnels and flight simulators.

Monte Carlo simulation is a technique named after the roulette wheels in Monte Carlo, which are seen as a device for generating random numbers. Using random numbers to assist with evaluating risk in capital investments was first suggested by David Hertz of the consulting firm McKinsey & Co in 1979. The uncertainties affecting the success or failure of a project are quantified using probability distributions. During the simulation, a large number of scenarios are created by sampling the probabilities at random to create a possible outcome for the project, and each project outcome is evaluated. The result is a probability distribution of possible outcomes for the project, expressed, for example, as an expected value of the net present value of the project, the range of possible outcomes and the downside risk of the project.

Most simulation models used in business are computerized (Monte Carlo) mathematical models, whose purpose is to recreate reality, in order to assess how future events might turn out. They can provide a wealth of information about how the future could differ from expectation, and allow management to analyse the risk in the situation. For example, management might use a financial simulation model to assess whether their company will achieve its risk-management target of financial survival or controlling costs, or a target for growth in profits.

A random-number simulation model consists of a number of interrelated variables. Some of the variables will have a range of possible values that can be represented by a probability distribution. Each possible outcome is allocated a range of random-number values. Other variables might have a value that is controllable by management, such as the price of a product or service delivered by the company. The model specifies how the variables inter-relate with each other to produce an outcome.

Once a model has been constructed, it can be used to analyse a large number of random outcomes. For controllable variables, the model user decides the value. For non-controllable variables, a value is generated through random numbers. The computer generates a random number, and the value assigned to the variable is the one to which the random number has been allocated. The variables in the model then interact to produce an outcome. Simulation modelling is an iterative process. Once one outcome has been produced, different random numbers are generated to produce another possible outcome, and so on. In this way, a large number of different possible outcomes are produced. These can then be analysed to assess the risks in the situation.

A simple example might help to illustrate simulation modelling. In practice, a model will usually be much more complex, and consist of many more controllable and non-controllable variables.

Suppose that each week a UK trading company buys a batch of products from a Belgian supplier, paying cash for the purchase. The products are priced in euros, but the price varies up and down each week. They are sold immediately to buyers in the USA, where they are priced in dollars. The volume of sales demand will depend on the dollar sales price, and the company has estimated the possible volumes of demand at a number of different price levels. US buyers are given credit. When they eventually pay, the income is exchanged for sterling at the spot rate. Probability estimates for the non-controllable variables are as follows:

Product purchase price			Credit taken by customer		
€	Probability	Random number allocation	Days	Probability	Random number allocation
70	0.2	00 – 19	40	0.5	00 – 49
71	0.4	20 – 59	50	0.3	50 – 79
72	0.4	60 – 99	60	0.2	80 – 99

Sales demand if product priced at $80			Sales demand if product priced at $85		
Demand	Prob	Random number allocation	Demand	Prob	Random number allocation
4,000	0.30	00 – 29	3,000	0.40	00 – 39
4,500	0.55	30 – 84	3,250	0.35	40 – 74
5,000	0.15	85 – 99	3,500	0.25	75 – 99

Daily movement in €/$ exchange rate			Daily movement in €/$ exchange rate		
Demand	Prob	Random number allocation	Demand	Prob	Random number allocation
- 0.02	0.10	00 – 09	- 0.04	0.05	00 – 04
- 0.01	0.20	10 – 29	- 0.02	0.20	05 – 24
0	0.35	30 – 64	0	0.35	25 – 59
+ 0.01	0.25	65 – 89	+ 0.02	0.25	60 – 84
+ 0.02	0.10	90 – 99	+ 0.04	0.15	85 – 99

The controllable variable here is the sales price, which could be either $80 or $85. Other variables in the model to which a starting value would be assigned could be the trader's opening cash position, and the opening exchange rates.

To run the model, the user should select a price. The model will then generate a series of random numbers, for purchase price, sales volume, exchange rates and length of credit period each week, over a budget period, say of one year. The outcomes produced will include estimates of weekly profitability and cash flows. The model can then be run several times over, with each iteration representing one budget period. Having analysed results with a selling price at $80, the model user can then do a similar exercise, with the price altered to $85.

Even with this relatively simple illustration, it might be apparent that a computerized simulation model is capable of producing a substantial amount of data for analysis, which can be used for risk management as well as planning purposes.

Problems with simulation modelling

There are some problems with simulation modelling that need to be recognized. The value of any information produced by a mathematical model is only as good as the model itself. Output should be interpreted with a full understanding of what basic assumptions have been used, and how reliable they are. In the example above, the possible values for purchase price, sales demand, exchange rate movements and credit period, or the associated probabilities, might all be unreliable. The model might also exclude variables that could be significant, such as the possibility that a customer will refuse to pay a debt for items purchased, or that there might be a supply shortage of the product in some weeks.

Analysing the data might also present a problem. A model can be used many times over to produce a wide range of possible outcomes, but the data produced has to be analysed and condensed into a comprehensible and usable form. A model cannot predict what the outcome will be, but can provide insights and help managers to understand the situation better.

3.9   Scenario planning

When senior managers assess the nature of strategic risk facing their company, they often do not consider the future objectively, but instead apply the subjective viewpoints of other people and a general consensus. There is an 'official' version of what conditions are likely to apply in the future, and so what could go wrong. Scenario planning is a methodology for planning the official view of future events by creating convincing alternatives and *looking at these alternatives in detail.*

It is argued that decision-makers evaluate risks largely be engaging in collective self-delusion. They start out with the accepted general view or collective wisdom, and do not challenge this view. In scenario planning, the 'official view' of the future should be one of the scenarios considered. It is not until this official scenario is convincingly challenged that decision-makers will consider other possible eventualities.

The planner therefore needs to establish what the generally accepted view of the future by interviewing and questioning decision-makers.

As an example of how the collective view can lead to bad strategic decisions, it is instructive to look at the case of AT&T in the USA in the late 1980s. In the late 1980s, the US government was heavily involved in administering the Internet, but wanted to withdraw from this role. The government therefore offered AT&T, as the largest long-distance telephone company in the USA, the role of administering the Internet. AT&T would not have to pay anything to take on this role. In effect, the US government was offering AT&T a monopoly control over the Internet over what was to become the driving force behind developments in communications in the 1990s. AT&T declined the government's offer.

Here was an example of decision-making that had a serious adverse strategic impact on a company, because it failed to seize the upside potential of an opportunity that was offered. The reason why AT&T turned down the US government's offer was the view of the future held by decision-makers at the top of the company. They could not see the potential of the new technology. AT&T had designed and built the switched network on which its telephony service operated, and their technical experts believed that packet switching, the technology on which the Internet operates, was inferior and would not work. The company could also see little demand for Internet services. The company's conclusion was that the Internet had no relevance to their own technology and little prospect for commercial success in its own right.

Scenario planners would argue that if AT&T had considered other scenarios in addition to the 'common viewpoint', they might have reached a different conclusion. For example, at that time a report prepared for the US government had been published suggesting that the Internet could change the face of telephony. Although the report was not accepted by everyone, it was sufficiently credible for planners to have considered a scenario in which the reports predictions turned out to be correct. AT&T also overlooked the developments that had already occurred in business-to-business electronic commerce to draw up a scenario in which the Internet could provide a medium for the expansion of online business.

If AT&T had used scenario planning, it could have built up an alternative plan for what should be done if Internet technology became important. Even if AT&T had decided not to accept the government's offer of an Internet monopoly, scenario planning would have made the company better prepared for the changes that did occur. Planning for the unlikely outcome would have helped the company to be on the look out for the early signs of change, and to be in a position to respond quickly when the unexpected happened. AT&T could have had a contingency plan for the Internet, and would have been able to challenge computer networking companies such as Cisco and Internet service providers such as AOL in the early days of market growth.

It could be argued that scenario planning is unnecessary, and that a company can change its strategy quickly. In the case of AT&T, senior management could have been alerted to the growing potential of the Internet by its technical experts. Scenario planning, however, offers the additional advantage of making the company think through the consequences of unexpected developments in some detail. A more detailed understanding of the unexpected means that decisions can be taken with a more informed judgement.

3.10   Value-at-risk

Value-at-risk is a technique for describing risk through a single number. It is a risk-measurement methodology used extensively in banks and has been strongly supported by banking regulators. Value-at-risk, or VaR, is obtained by looking at the probability distribution of possible losses over a specified future time period, and identifying the maximum loss at a given level of probability. The probability level used is typically 95%, so VaR is a measure of the maximum loss the organization would expect to incur from unexpected events, at a 95% level of probability, over a time period of, say, one day or two weeks.

VaR is not a maximum possible loss. It is the maximum loss that will occur 95% of the time. If a 5% probability of a higher loss is a matter of concern for the organization, it can use a tighter measure of VaR and specify the maximum loss that is expected at a 99% probability level.

An advantage of VaR is that it converts everything into a money measure, and can be applied to all kinds of financial positions, in equities, bonds, currencies, options and other derivatives.

The use of probability distributions to measure risk might seem familiar if you know about normal distributions and standard deviations. VaR is not, however, a normal curve distribution analysis. In a normal curve, values above and below the average are a mirror image of each other, and the probability of loss is matched by an equal probability of gain. With a VaR model, this is not the case. The model has to allow for option positions in which the upside potential for an option holder is unlimited and the downside restricted to the cost of the option. For an option writer, the upside is limited to the option premium income, but the downside risk is much greater.

In 1996, the capital adequacy rules applied to international banks were changed, and banks were required to hold a minimum amount of capital to cover the market risks on their trading positions. The need to measure market risks gave impetus to the development of internal risk systems by banks to calculate their VaR. For banks, there has been the incentive that a sophisticated risk-measurement system should give them an opportunity to measure their risk more accurately, and so have a lower regulatory capital requirement than if they applied more general and standardized rules for measuring market risk. At about the same time, the investment bank J P Morgan made its own VaR model freely available to other financial institutions. VaR models based on the J P Morgan model are now widely used.

VaR models often use simplifying assumptions about risk, and are by no means perfect in measuring risk. Nevertheless, they provide a useful and simple methodology. VaR summarizes the downside risk in a market portfolio in a single number. If, for example, a bank states that its VaR is $25 million, this will mean that for 95% of the time it does not expect to lose more than $25 million in one day's trading.

3.11   Conclusion

Risk analysis calls for a measurement of risks, and provides a basis for prioritizing risks in order of significance. Statistical methods can be used to obtain estimates of potential loss or gain, and the analysis process can involve complex mathematics to analyse loss probabilities, the impact of adverse outcomes, ranges in possible outcomes and volatility. Many organizations use modelling to analyse risks. In the financial markets, for example, insurance companies use statistical analysis to predict risk losses, and banks use models for analysing their exposures to risks.

However, analysis does not have to be numbers-based, and judgements based on knowledge or experience can be used to measure risks. Smaller companies in particular are likely to use a probability/impact matrix for risk mapping, rather than mathematical analysis.

At the end of the risk analysis process, management should have an understanding of the significant risks facing the company, what the possible loss or gain could be in each case, and the frequency or probability of different possible outcomes. The next stage in the risk management process is to consider controls for each risk.

Everyone takes on risks. The secret of mastering risk is to identify them, analyse them carefully and mitigate downside risks as far as it is possible and economical to do so. The remaining risks should be monitored and controlled, ensuring that contingency plans are in place should a risk event occur. Doing this will increase the chances of success.

4

CONTROL OF RISK

After reading this chapter, you should:

- Be able to explain the risk-management process and the roles of the people responsible

- Understand the various controls that might be applied to different types of risk

- Understand how controls are imposed and monitored, and periodically evaluated and tested

- Understand the costs and benefits of risk-control measures.

4.1   The risk-management process

Spreading risk to reduce exposure

Large companies are no longer prepared to approach risk management on a risk-by-risk basis. For example, there is no point in protecting a building against the risk of damage by purchasing insurance for £10 million when potential risks of £15 million from adverse currency movements go unmanaged.

Entity-wide risk management is based on the methods described in the previous chapter, which have the following features:

- Risk identification.

- Risk assessment. Risks are assessed for frequency and severity.

- Risk consolidation. Once a risk has been assessed, it is put on a risk map, and the company is able to see the nature of all the major risks that it faces.

- Risk portfolio management. The risks are then assessed as a whole. The company should be considered as a set of value propositions for investors and as a portfolio of risks that amounts to the value presented to the investors. It must then manage the return earned by the company relative to the risks taken on to obtain the return.

The advantages of a portfolio approach to risk management

Large companies should have an *integrated approach* to the management of its risks, and should apply a consistent policy for risk control and containment to its entire portfolio of risks. There are several benefits to be obtained from an integrated enterprise-wide approach.

- There is no sense in taking measures to control one particular significant risk if no measures are taken to control other risks of equal significance. If an organization limits its exposure to some risks but not others of the same significance, it cannot consider itself adequately protected.

- There could be offsetting risks, particularly with exposures to financial risk. If these are dealt with on an enterprise-wide basis, they can be set off against each other, and the risk avoided at no cost. Suppose for example that a UK group of companies includes two subsidiaries, one that is owed €5 million by a customer and one that owes €5 million to a customer, with both debts payable on the same date in the future. Taken separately, each subsidiary has an exposure to a change in the exchange rate for euro/sterling, and if the risks are dealt with individually, each subsidiary might take measures to hedge the risk. On an enterprise-wide basis, however, the asset of €5 million and the liability of €5 million offset each other, and the group has no net exposure at all. As a consequence, there is no risk that has to be hedged.

- There can be savings from economies of scale in purchasing insurance. For example, a company might have twenty buildings, for each of which property insurance is required. The cost of insuring the twenty properties all together under the same policy will probably be much less than if they are insured separately.

A company should also be aware of its overall risk profile, and it is the responsibility of the board of directors to ensure that the total risks facing the company are consistent with the company's aims and strategies.

By looking at risks on an aggregate basis, managers get a much better understanding of how the business works and how it operates as a whole. An integrated approach also encourages an innovative attitude to risk management, and encourages companies to look for new ways of managing risks. It can also help a company to plan a more efficient insurance programme, partly by purchasing insurance in bulk at lower premiums and partly by increasing the amount of self-insurance.

The danger in managing with individual risks separately

A danger with managing risks individually is that once one particular type of risk has been identified and dealt with, the risk could move towards something else that has not been identified and is not properly managed. A major example is the collapse of the hedge fund Long-Term Capital Management (LTCM) in 1998. LTCM took highly-leveraged positions in equities, focusing on risk-management measures to protect the company from market risk (price risk) in its investment positions. The problem was that in building up its investment positions, the company ignored a different risk, liquidity risk. Prices in the markets turned against LTCM. Its managers had been ready for this eventuality and had planned to sell off investments as soon as the problem emerged. However, when they tried to sell, they found themselves unable to liquidate the positions quickly enough, suffering huge losses as a result that led to financial collapse.

Another example is the syndicated lending by US banks to emerging markets during the early 1980s. The banks were eager to lend, but wanted to protect themselves against the risk from adverse currency movements and interest rate movements. They therefore insisted on dollar-denominated lending (to avoid currency risk) and floating-rate loans (to avoid interest-rate risk). US interest rates soared in the early 1980s, and the dollar appreciated in value. Countries such as Mexico and Brazil were unable to meet the higher loan payments and defaulted. By protecting themselves from currency and interest rate risk, the US banks had exposed themselves to credit risk.

Since controlling risk can simply lead to the creation of other risks, the only protection is to adopt an enterprise-wide risk-management approach (ERM), or integrated risk management, which aims to measure, control and manage all risks of the organization across all risk categories and product lines. Techniques for quantifying and analysing risks, adopted from insurance risk and financial risk management, have made this possible.

Risk avoidance and risk acceptance: risk control and risk containment

- Having identified and prioritized risks and analysed the 'gross risk' facing the organization, the next stage in an integrated risk management process is to formulate strategies for risk avoidance and acceptance, and for risk control and containment. 'Gross risk' is a term for the amount of loss (or gain) to which a company is exposed from a particular risk, on the assumption that no measures are taken to control or contain it.

- 'Net risk' or *residual risk* is the amount of loss or gain to which a company is exposed after avoidance, control or containment measures have been taken.

Risk avoidance is to prevent any exposure to risk, and is the complete opposite of risk acceptance. Risks are avoided by not getting into a situation where unexpected losses might be suffered,. For example, a company might avoid exposure to risk from economic conditions in South America by refusing to invest in South America at all.

Risk acceptance means tolerating an exposure to risk. If the risk is not significant, management might do nothing about it, except keep it under watch to make sure that it does not get more serious over time. Alternatively, risks might be accepted, but measures taken to reduce the risk in some way, through risk control or risk containment. **Risk controls** are measures to reduce the size of an exposure to a risk by limiting the potential loss (ie limiting the gross risk). **Risk containment** refers to measures for reducing the remaining exposures, through techniques for risk sharing, risk transfer or some form of insurance.

4.2 The persons responsible for risk management

The **board of directors** has the ultimate responsibility for risk management in a company, and should formulate a risk management strategy. For each exposure, the directors should decide whether they are prepared to accept the gross risk. If they are not prepared to accept the gross risk, they should consider a strategy for avoiding or reducing the gross risk through control or containment. The board's responsibility for risk management is a feature of corporate governance, and is explained more fully in a later chapter.

The board decides the overall risk management strategy that management will implement. **Management** will formulate the detailed strategy and will be responsibility for and accountable for maintaining and monitoring the controls. In practice, the chief executive will usually be given the overall responsibility, and will delegate responsibilities to other executives.

Having formulated and applied an approach to risk management, the managers responsible should continue to monitor the situation, quantifying the net risk or residual risk regularly, and reporting to the board. The board should decide whether the residual risk is at a sensible and acceptable level, or whether the risk reduction measures should be redesigned. The board should also be satisfied that effective early warning mechanisms for unexpected events are in place for each of the significant risks.

Procedural and rule-based controls

When the system of control is based on rules and procedures, individuals are made responsible for ensuring that particular controls are applied when carrying out an activity, and the work done by one person is often checked or authorized by someone else. For example, in order to incur expenditure, an employee might be required to submit a request form, which will then be authorized by a supervisor or manager, and if the expense exceeds a certain amount of money, a second authorization might be required, from a more senior person. In the financial markets, deals made by a trader are subsequently checked by 'back office' staff, and also confirmed with the other party to the trade.

A risk-based management approach to controls

Procedural controls are essential in some areas, particularly to prevent fraud and to safeguard assets. A risk-based management approach makes use of procedural controls, but also goes beyond them and seeks to instil a culture of risk awareness within the organization. The risk-management process becomes embedded in the management processes in the company.

Although managers are accountable for controlling risks for which they are responsible, all staff should be involved in the risk-management process, and should be informed by senior management about the company's risk-management policy, the key business objectives and significant business risks facing the business. There should also be clear communication to staff of the company's policy on risk management.

The aim should be to improve the risk awareness culture at all levels within the organization, and attitudes to risk management and internal controls.

● Individuals should be encouraged to report problems rather than sit on them.

- Staff might also be involved in the regular cycle of risk identification and control. Round tables or workshops should be held regularly to discuss risk and internal control at a local level. Employees might even be given training in business risk.

Some organizations employ risk managers, whose responsibility is not just to arrange insurance on a group-wide basis, but also to discuss ways of limiting the frequency or impact of risks with the managers responsible. Risk managers can therefore have an advisory role in the process. Similarly, organizations might employ internal auditors to monitor controls and risks, and to report back to management with advice or suggestions for improvements.

Fundamentals of good risk management and internal control

Managers are responsible for achieving the fundamental requirements for a sound system of risk management and internal control, which are as follows:

- There must be an awareness of risk.

- There must also be an awareness of the objectives of the company.

- Fundamental controls, such as financial controls, should be applied and effective.

- There should be consultation throughout the company on risk management and controls.

- Decision-making should be based on reliable business information.

- Control strategies must be applied continually.

- There must be an emphasis on changing the culture of the company and the behaviour of employees.

- There should be early warning systems in place, and quick response when warnings occur.

- The control system should be simple and understandable.

In smaller listed companies, the board of directors might discuss risk more frequently than the board of a large public company, because the board generally meets more often and because the directors normally have more of a hands-on approach to the running of the company. In small companies, the executive directors hold many of the senior executive management posts. In contrast, the board in a larger company will rely more heavily on its executive management team.

4.3   Risk controls

Risk controls are measures taken by an organization to:

- prevent or eliminate events where losses occur

- reduce the frequency of losses (**loss prevention**)

- reduce the severity or impact of losses that do occur (**loss reduction**)

- enhance the possibility of gains, or even

- exploit opportunities to maximize gains.

It is arguable that another important aspect of risk control is the reduction of uncertainty. Uncertainty is created by a lack of information about risk, and is reduced by improving the quality and timeliness of information for decision-making.

Although many controls are voluntary, some are obligatory and must achieve at least a minimum level of acceptability. These include controls to ensure health and safety at work. Some risks are avoidable, and an organization can choose to prevent any exposure to particular risks. Other risks are unavoidable, and the choice for the organization is to accept the gross risk, or to reduce the risk to a residual amount, by reducing their frequency or impact, or by adopting other risk-containment measures such as insurance.

The approach to dealing with pure risk will vary according to the severity and the frequency of the risk. The following matrix suggests a general policy for risk management, but the actual measures taken in any situation (acceptance, control or containment) will depend on circumstances and risk attitudes.

		Severity/impact	
		Low	**High**
Frequency/ probability	**Low**	Accept the risk. The cost of mitigating the risk is likely to exceed the benefits. Keep the risk under periodic review.	Insure the risk, or develop a contingency plan. Try to reduce the impact of losses, should they occur. (For insured risks, this will mean lower insurance premiums.)
	High	Consider measures to control by reducing its frequency, or risk - containment measures.	Measures to control or contain the risk must be taken.

4.4   Types of control

Controls can be categorized in different ways, and the type of control or controls to apply to any risk will depend on the nature of the risk. Three broad classifications of control are physical controls, system controls and management controls.

A large variety of **physical controls** are used to protect people, money and other assets. People might be protected by protection suits and helmets when they are working in a dangerous environment, by safety belts when they are driving, by guard rails around machinery to prevent accidents, and so on. Cash might be protected physically by locking it away in a safe. Physical assets might be given protective covering, and access to certain assets might be protected by security measures such as locks, alarms, security guards and closed circuit television cameras.

System controls include procedural controls, organization controls, software controls and financial controls. **Procedural controls** are established ways of performing activities, to ensure that work is done to a proper standard and errors are detected at an early stage. Work procedures might be organized so that work done by one person is checked by someone else. **Organization controls** are created by the structure of authority, responsibility and accountability within the organization. Individuals are given authority and responsibility for certain decisions. Decisions, such as spending decisions, have to be authorized by an appropriate individual. The delegation of authority means that managers are able to use some initiative, and take controlled risks where an opportunity arises for making gains or avoiding unnecessary losses.

Software controls are written into computer systems to protect the system from errors in processing, loss of data and unauthorized access. Controls include measures for data file security, passwords to prevent unauthorized access and virus software to protect data from corruption.

Financial controls are controls of a financial nature providing financial protection. Within the banking industry, for example, a well-established method of controlling credit risk is taking security for loans. In the foreign exchange markets and money markets, risk can be reduced by using forward contracts. Financial controls are also imposed by regulation. Banks, for example, are required to maintain a minimum amount of their own capital to support their business operations, to protect customer deposits and other creditors of the bank in the event of the bank making large losses.

Management controls are controls applied by management. They include the formulation of strategies for the control of risk. All planning measures, for example, are a form of risk control, because plans are intended to ensure, if they are successfully achieved, that the organization will achieve its aims and objectives. The approval of the annual budget by the board of directors should be a major element in risk management control within every company. More specifically, contingency plans are back-up measures in the event of a catastrophe.

It was suggested earlier that measures to **improve the quality of information** are an important form of risk control, because better-quality information reduces the amount of uncertainty in decision-making. Another aspect of information control are controls over the announcements of information by an organization to the public at large. Companies often use public relations specialists to promote or protect their image (ie **control reputational risk**) and hire firms to lobby government in the interests of the company. 'Spin doctoring' might have a bad name, because it is associated in the public mind with the presentation of information rather than the content. However, control by companies over the publication of financially-sensitive information can be essential to protect investors against profiteering by individuals with insider knowledge, and there are strict regulations for listed companies about making announcements.

Manual and automated controls

Another helpful way of classifying controls is to distinguish between manual and automated controls. Manual controls require human intervention to ensure that the control is applied, and as such the risk of a failure in the control system might be higher.

4.5 Control strategy and systems

Control strategy

A control strategy determines the broad approach to controlling particular risks. Once a strategy has been decided, management can devise the detailed controls.

An initial strategic choice might be a decision whether or not to take on a risk at all. Risk can be eliminated from an operation by exiting the business. If a particular area of operations has become too risky, or provides low returns for the amount of capital employed, an *exit strategy* would allow the organization to switch resources to other operations where the risks are lower or the returns higher.

Where a risk is accepted, a strategy for controlling or containing the risk should be decided. For example, suppose that a company considers that its business is exposed to risk from poor quality service to customers and measures must be taken to maintain quality standards at or above a certain level. Depending on the detailed circumstances of the situation, a variety of quality control strategies might be considered, such as greater automation, closer supervision of work procedures or better employee training and selecting only its best people to deal directly with customers.

Internal control system

Internal control is an essential element within a risk management system. The term 'internal control system', as used by accountants, means a combination of the control environment and control policies and procedures within an organization. The control environment refers to the overall attitude of directors and management towards internal controls, their awareness of the controls and the actions they take to apply controls. It is important because it sets the overall style and culture of the organization in its approach to the management of risk.

Internal controls are all the policies and procedures applied to ensure that the organization conducts its business in an orderly and efficient way. This includes measures to prevent and detect fraud, safeguard the assets of the business, and achieve adherence to internal policies, the accuracy and completeness of accounting records and the timely preparation of reliable financial information. Although internal controls are often associated with the accounting system in an organization, they extend much more widely.

Audit of the control system

The system within an organization for managing and controlling risk could be inadequate, for either of two reasons. Firstly, the controls that have been established might be ignored or avoided. Secondly, the controls that are applied properly might be inadequate for dealing with the risks. An inadequate control system is much more likely to exist in organizations where a culture of risk awareness is missing, but weaknesses can arise in any organization.

Within a company, the board of directors should satisfy itself that the control system is functioning properly and is effective. One way of obtaining this reassurance is to obtain regular reports from management, but a weakness of management reports is that they cannot be objective, because they are prepared by the individuals responsible for the application of the controls. Another way of obtaining reassurance is to carry out an independent investigation ('audit') into the control systems and risk management.

Companies are required by law to carry out an independent investigation into their financial control systems each year. This investigation is made annually by the company's external auditors, who check the accounting records and the annual financial statements of the company. They then prepare a report to the shareholders on whether the financial statements give a 'true and fair view' of the financial performance of the company for the year and its financial position at the year-end. The auditors' report is included in the published report and accounts of the company.

The checks carried out by the external auditors do not cover all aspects of internal control and risk management, particularly non-accounting aspects of risk. A company might therefore carry out additional investigations of its own, using internal auditors. Internal auditors are simply in-house investigators who ought to be independent from the executive management responsible for the systems they investigate. An internal audit team might do work similar to the checking performed by the external auditors, and in cooperation with the external auditors. In addition, however, internal auditors might carry out investigations into any particular aspect of control and risk management.

Periodic evaluation and testing of controls

Risks should be monitored and managed, and audit work on its own is insufficient. The board of directors of a company should have regular assurance that the system of internal control is functioning efficiently and effectively, and that risks are being properly identified and managed. There are several possible sources of such assurance.

As explained above, the external auditors should provide reassurance about the accuracy of the accounting records and the reliability of the financial statements. However, the external auditors report officially to the shareholders. The boards of UK listed companies are expected to establish a professional dialogue with the external auditors through their audit committee.

The internal audit department, if there is one, might produce reports for the board or the audit committee. Alternatively, specific studies and risk reviews might be commissioned from external consultants, such as a firm of management consultants.

Management might be required to report to the board regularly on aspects of control, and provide confirmation that the controls are in place and properly applied, and that they function effectively. Alternatively, the board might obtain similar reassurance from reports by either the chief executive (or managing director) or the finance director.

Where possible, the board should ensure that early-warning mechanisms are in place, to provide prompt notification when a control or risk limit has been breached. These might be financial warnings, such as reports indicating that borrowing covenants will be breached, or that there could soon be a shortage of cash. Early-warning mechanisms can also be provided by other types of control, such as physical controls or software controls. For example, a security alarm system might be installed to give warning when an intruder has breached a perimeter fence, and temperature gauges are used to give early warning of overheating in equipment.

There should be regular formal reviews by the board of the risk-management process within the company. This should include a review of the procedures for risk identification, assessment and analysis. The review should address high-level risks at a strategic level as well as risks at an operational level.

The pitfalls to effective risk management and internal control

A risk-based management process can fail for a variety of reasons.

The board might fail to give proper consideration to strategic, high-level risks. An example might help to illustrate this point. Suppose that a UK-based company manufactures a range of products that are sold mainly to countries in the euro zone, and the prices at which the products have to be sold in European markets makes it difficult for the company to make much profit. The company would be exposed to currency risk because its costs are in sterling and its revenues in euros. The board should consider long-term measures to reduce the risk, possible by transferring production into the euro zone. If the board did not give at least serious consideration to the risks from currency exposure, it would be failing to address a key strategic issue.

The board of directors cannot get operational managers to 'buy into' the risk-management process. Unless the board can gain the backing of management, it will be impossible to create a risk-aware culture within the organization. Managers might even fail to carry out their basic responsibilities for ensuring that basic controls are properly applied, without which control systems cannot possibly be effective.

Even when the board and management pay lip service to the necessity for a risk-management system, they might give insufficient attention in practice to the fundamentals of effective risk management – identification, assessment analysis, controls and containment, together with regular audits and reviews. In some cases, a risk-control system might become a burdensome bureaucracy, stifling initiative and enterprise.

There might be no early warning mechanisms, so that when an unexpected event occurs, its impact is unexpected and disruptive. Even when risks are identified, an organization might be slow to react to them, and problems might be left too late before they are dealt with.

On the other hand, there could be a system weakness from risk identification overload. If too many risks are identified for assessment, it will become difficult to identify and manage the significant risks.

4.6   Costs and benefits of risk control measures

Risks have a potential cost, but so too do measures to control risks. The cost of control should be compared with the expected benefits. As a general principle, unless the benefits are worth more than the cost, the control measure cannot be justified. However, although this principle might seem straightforward, it might not be so easily applied in practice. There are three reasons for this.

- It is difficult to measure accurately the potential loss or gain that could occur as a result of an exposure to risk if no control measures are taken. The previous chapter on risk analysis explained that for a pure risk, the potential loss from an unexpected event might be calculated as the expected value of the loss, which is an estimated probability of the loss multiplied by an estimate of the severity of the loss should it occur. The measures of probability and severity are both estimates, possibly based on historical averages.

- The benefit of control action might be to reduce, but not eliminate, the risk. It could be very difficult to assess by how much the potential loss or gain is affected by a control measure. Any estimates of the potential loss or gain from speculative risk would also be based on estimates and probabilities, rather than certain values.

- The potential losses or gains from an exposure to risk, and the benefits of a control, cannot all be measured in money terms. Some control measures affect employee attitudes (for example, measures to improve safety or security at work) or the reputation of the organization (for example, control measures that show concern for protection of the environment). Even so, the non-monetary benefits from risk control measures can be substantial, and should not be ignored in formulating risk-control measures.

In spite of the problems with measuring risk costs and control benefits, cost benefit analysis can sometimes be used to decide whether a particular control measure is justified. The following examples are illustrative only.

Example 1

Suppose that a supermarket estimates that its losses from theft of goods by customers is in the region of £1 million each year, measured in terms of purchase cost of the items. There is no insurance against the losses. The manager of the supermarket has estimated that losses would be reduced by about 10% if two extra security guards were recruited. The total cost of the security guards would be £75,000 each year. If the manager's estimates are correct, losses from theft would be reduced by about £100,000 for an expenditure of £75,000, leaving the company better off by £25,000 each year. Against this would be set the potential risk to the supermarket's reputation from any additional incidents involving the detention of innocent customers.

Example 2

Suppose that in order to cover the cost of its own funding and make a suitable profit margin, a bank needs to earn an interest rate of 6.75% on one-year loans to small corporate customers. However, the bank knows from past experience that the likelihood of default on unsecured one-year loans to small corporates is 10%, and the recovery value of these loans will be nil. In order to obtain a net return of 6.75%, allowing for the losses from defaults, the bank would have to charge interest of (6.75/90%) 7.50% on its loans to these customers. In contrast, suppose that if the loans are secured and the recovery value in an event of default is 100%, the interest rate the bank would have to charge would be 6.75%. In this rather simplified example, it should be apparent that a bank can calculate the effect of taking security on loans, and the reduction in expected losses will be reflected in a lower interest rate to the customer.

4.7   Conclusion

This chapter has focused on risk controls to reduce the severity and frequency of possible losses (or increase the opportunities for gain), on the assumption that the organization retains the exposures. Procedural control systems are inevitably a key element in risk control.

Some residual risks that remained despite control measures might be transferred, insured by a third party or shared. These types of risk management action (risk containment) are considered in the next chapter.

5

CONTAINMENT OF RISK

After reading this chapter, you should:

● Be able to explain the principle of risk containment and the nature of risk retention, risk transfer, risk neutralization and risk sharing

● Understand the nature of pooling and hedging as methods of risk neutralization

● Understand how risk can be transferred, through insurance, forward contracts, securitization and derivative instruments

● Understand the nature of insurance and, in broad outline, insurance contracts

● Understand how forward contracts can be used to transfer risk

● Understand the nature of securitization

● Understand, in broad terms, various types of financial derivatives and how these can be used to transfer risk (hedge exposures)

● Appreciate the need to plan a strategy for risk control and containment.

5.1   Risk control and risk containment

Measures to **control downside risk** seek to **avoid a risk entirely**, reduce the frequency of loss events (**loss prevention**) or reduce the magnitude of a risk (**loss reduction**). When exposures to a risk are reduced through control measures, there will usually be some residual risk.

Risk containment is a term for measures to keep residual risks within acceptable limits, so that the organization will be better able to survive an adverse event. Risk containment measures include **risk neutralization**, **risk sharing**, and the **transfer of risk**, for example through **insurance**.

Risk control measures	Risk containment measures
Risk avoidance	Neutralization
Loss prevention (reduce loss frequency)	Risk sharing
Loss reduction (reduce impact of losses)	Risk transfer
	Insurance

The basic principles of risk control and containment can be summarized as follows:

- Identify and analyse significant risks for the organization.

- For each significant risk, develop a strategy for management.

- An organization might decide to avoid some risks altogether, perhaps by exiting from an area of operations where the risks do not seem justified by the expected returns.

- For the risks that remain, control measures should be considered, to reduce the frequency or magnitude of potential losses.

- With control measures in place, there will still be some residual risk for the organization, for which a management strategy should be formulated.

- If the residual risk is insignificant, due to the effectiveness of risk control measures, the organization might decide that the risk is bearable, and no further measures are necessary.

- If the residual risk is still potentially significant, the organization should consider ways of containing the risk, so that it will be better able to survive an adverse event.

5.2   Risk retention and risk transfer

Risk retention refers to methods of risk containment where an organization bears the risk itself, and if an adverse outcome occurs, it will suffer the full amount of the loss itself. **Risk transfer** refers to methods of shifting the cost of the risk to an unrelated third party, such as an insurance company. (A third method of containing risk, risk neutralization, is explained later.)

The distinction between risk transfer and risk retention is by no means clear cut, and containment measures generally include some element of retention and some of transfer. This is apparent even with insurance policies. An insurance policy transfers the economic risk to the insurance company, but the actual risk remains with the policyholder. For example, when a company buys insurance against theft of equipment, it will suffer any actual loss from theft, but the insurance policy provides protection against the economic loss incurred. When an organization buys insurance from an independent insurance company, it must also pay regular premiums. The insurance company will set the premiums at a level where it will expect the income from the premiums to cover the cost of all expected insurance claims (in other words, all expected future losses of policyholders) and make some profit. An organization buying insurance is really therefore just spreading the cost of expected future losses more evenly over time, by paying insurance policy premiums.

5.3   Risk retention and self-insurance

If an organization does not take any measures to contain a risk through transfer or neutralization, it is retaining the risk, and will have to accept the full economic consequence of any loss that occurs.

- To some extent, all organizations practice some degree of risk retention, partly because they are unaware in advance of some of the risk to which they are exposed, and so do not take any measures to deal with it. The risk might become apparent only when it is the cause of an unexpected loss.

- A second reason for risk retention is that the residual risk might be fairly small, and containment measures are therefore considered unnecessary.

- A third reason might be that the expected benefits from risk containment are not justified by the cost of any measures that would need to be taken. For example, a company might decide against key man insurance for its chief executive, because the cost of the premium would be too high.

When a residual risk exists and is recognized, but the organization takes no measures to contain the risk, it is practising **self-insurance**. As the term suggests, the organization effectively acts as its own insurance company, and it accepts that if any loss is incurred, it will bear the economic cost itself.

Most companies bear their strategic risks and many business risks. For example, some years ago, a major publishing group made the strategic decision to invest heavily in electronic publishing for legal and scientific titles. There was considerable risk in the strategy, whose success depended on the popularity with customers of on-line access to the titles, but it was a risk that the group had to take on itself. The risks could be controlled to some extent, by taking measures to improve the chances of success with the venture, through careful attention to product quality and vigorous marketing efforts. By bearing the risk, the group hoped to benefit from future profits from a successful strategic initiative.

In the same way, companies have to bear the business risk of sales revenues being lower or higher than expected, or of a new product being more or less successful than anticipated. These risks can be controlled through initiatives such as rigorous new product design and testing, market research and advertising. These measures can reduce the probable impact of any disappointing outcome and increase the chances of a better-than-expected outcome. However, although the business risk can be controlled, it cannot be transferred to another party.

Some large organizations have formalized some aspects of self-insurance by establishing a **group insurance subsidiary**, from which other companies in the group are required to obtain their insurance cover. For example, ABC Group might establish a subsidiary, ABC Insurance Limited, and all the companies in the group would buy their insurance from the insurance subsidiary. The insurance subsidiary would operate in a similar way to an independent insurer, pooling the risks of its various customers, and charging premiums sufficient to cover the expected losses of the group and earn some profit. With an internal insurance subsidiary, the group bears the economic risk itself, and does not transfer it to an outside party.

A conscious decision to self-insure a risk will be based largely on two considerations:

● the extent to which the organization is able to control the risk

● the cost of risk transfer.

Control over the risk. As a general rule, self-insurance will be more attractive when the risk can be controlled with a reasonable amount of success. Suppose for example that you have a mortgage from your bank on your home, and you are offered insurance against the risk of losing your job through redundancy. If you are made redundant, the insurance company would pay the equivalent of your monthly salary for twelve months after you have left your job. You might decide to turn down the offer of insurance, because you believe that in the event of being made redundant, you would be able to find a new job within a month or so, and the cost of the insurance was therefore too much. You would have decided to retain the risk yourself, because you would have sufficient control over the situation if redundancy were to occur.

The cost of risk transfer. The cost of insurance will depend partly on the assessment of the risk by the insurance company and also the profit margin taken by the insurance company on the policies it writes. If a company makes a lower assessment cost than the insurance company of the cost of the risk, or if the insurance company would take a very high profit margin, the insurance premium might seem too high, making self-insurance (risk retention) a better choice.

5.4   Risk sharing

Risk can be partly retained and partly transferred to someone else, so that it is a shared risk. Risk sharing is a common feature of many insurance policies, such as car insurance, private medical insurance and home contents insurance, where the insurer agrees to pay any losses suffered by the policy holder in excess of a stated amount. For example, if the excess on a private medical insurance policy is £100 and the policy holder incurs medical expenses of £300, the insurance company will pay just £200. The main benefit of agreeing to an 'excess' on an insurance policy is that the cost of the insurer's premium will be lower.

In business, the sharing of strategic risk and business risk is evident in **joint ventures** and **partnerships**. Two or more independent companies might form a joint venture to undertake a project, providing capital and other resources, and sharing the profits, in a pre-agreed ratio. If the venture fails, the loss of each company will be limited to its share of the total. An important benefit of risk sharing through joint ventures or partnerships is that each partner can restrict its share of the total risk to what it considers affordable or bearable, and excessive exposure to a high-risk venture is contained.

Risk sharing is sometimes a strategic necessity. For example, most countries in Central and Eastern Europe, after the collapse of their communist regimes, were opened up to investment from western companies. Western companies often found that the most successful way of penetrating these markets was to establish joint ventures with domestic companies.

5.5 Risk neutralization: pooling and hedging

Neutralization of risk refers to measures that are intended to offset one risk with another, so that the risks tend to cancel each other out, leaving the actual outcome likely to be close to the expected outcome. Neutralization can include elements of both risk control and risk containment, and methods of neutralizing risk are **pooling** and **hedging**.

Pooling risks

Pooling risks involves building up a portfolio of risks such that, on the balance of probabilities, some events will turn out favourably and some adversely, but on average the actual outcome will be close to expectation. The concept of pooling is used by insurance companies. Insurance companies write policies on similar risks for a large number of different customers, in the expectation that there will be claims under some policies but not on others. Taken as a whole, pay-outs to cover the insured losses will be less than the total of the insurance premiums received. The pooling concept applies here because the actual losses for a large number of similar insured risks should be close to the average expected losses for those risks.

The same concept applies to building up an investment portfolio, or a portfolio of investment projects. Any individual investment could produce returns that are equal to, above or below expectation. By pooling investments into a large portfolio, some investments are likely to produce the expected return, others will provide a return in excess of expectation, and some will disappoint. Taken as a whole, the probability of large unexpected losses will be reduced, and actual returns are more likely to turn out close to expectation. A simple example might help to illustrate this point mathematically.

Suppose that a firm has two projects under consideration. Project A has a 50% probability of making a profit of £1,000 and a 50% probability of a loss of £600. Project B has a 50% probability of making a profit of £2,000 and a 50% probability of a loss of £800.

Probability	Project A	Project B
50%	+ £1,000	+ £2,000
50%	- £600	- £800

If the firm undertakes just one project and not the other, it would face a 50% probability of making a loss. The firm could create a portfolio of two projects by undertaking both of them, not just one.

The risk in each project might be **positively correlated**, which means that if project A makes a profit, project B is also likely to make a profit, and if one of the projects incurs a loss, the other is likely to do the same. With positively correlated returns, the possible outcomes would be as follows.

Probability	Projects A and B
50%	(+ £1,000 + £2,000) + £3,000
50%	(- £600 - £800) - £1,400

When project returns are positively correlated, there is no reduction in risk. Here, there is still a 50% probability of making a loss. The expected value of profit is £800 (50% of £3,000 plus 50% of - £1,400).

The risk in each project might be **negatively correlated**, which means that if project A makes a profit, project B is likely to make a loss, and if project B makes a profit, project A is likely to make a loss. With negatively correlated returns, the possible outcomes would be as follows:

Probability	Projects A and B
50%	(+ £1,000 - £800) + £200
50%	(+ £2,000 - £600) + £1,400

The maximum possible profit is less than when returns are positively correlated, but in this example, the worst possible outcome is a profit rather than a loss. The expected value of profit is still = £800 (50% of £1,400 + 50% of £200).

The returns from each project might have **no correlation whatsoever**, so that the probability of making a profit or loss on one project has no statistical relationship with the probability of a profit or loss on the other. The range of possible outcomes, and the probabilities of each outcome, are as follows:

Probability	Outcome		Expected value
			£
(0.5 x 0.5) 0.25	(+ £1,000 + £2,000)	+ £3,000	+ 750
(0.5 x 0.5) 0.25	(+ £1,000 - £800)	+ £200	+ 50
(0.5 x 0.5) 0.25	(+ £2,000 - £600)	+ £1,400	+ 350
(0.5 x 0.5) 0.25	(- £800 - £600)	- £1,400	- 350
			+ 800

The worst possible outcome is a loss of £1,400, but creating a portfolio of projects has reduced the probability of a loss from 50% to 25%, and has increased the probability of a profit from 50% to 75%. The expected value of the profit is again £800.

This example shows the effect on risk of creating a portfolio of just two investments. By building up a much larger portfolio, the risk will be reduced much further.

Hedging exposures to risk

Hedging risks means creating a position that offsets an exposure to a speculative risk by establishing a new risk in the opposite direction. When a hedge is 'perfect', an adverse outcome on one position is favourable will be matched by an equal favourable outcome on the other. Taken together, there will be neither an unexpected gain nor an unexpected loss. Derivative instruments such as futures and options can be used to hedge financial risks, and these are described later. Another hedging technique is **netting**, which is commonly used to hedge currency risk.

Currency risk can arise by having a future stream of income in a foreign currency, because there is a risk that the value of the currency will fall and the future income, when converted into domestic currency, will be worth less than expected. For example, suppose that a UK company expects to receive income of $15,000 each month for the next twelve months, and the current exchange rate is £1 = $1.50. The expected future income is therefore £10,000 each month, on the assumption that the exchange rate is unchanged. The company has an exposure to currency risk from its future dollar income. If the dollar were to fall in value against sterling, say to £1 = $1.60, the value in sterling of the monthly income would fall to £9,375.

Similarly, if a company expects to make future payments in a foreign currency, it will have an exposure to the risk of an increase in the value of that currency against its domestic currency. If a UK company expected to make payments of €15,000 each month for the next twelve months and the current exchange rate is £1 = €1.50, the expected monthly cost would be £10,000. However, if the euro strengthened to, say, £1 = €1.40, the cost would rise to £10,714.

With netting of income and expenditure, a company simply uses foreign currency income to make foreign currency payments, and to the extent that the income and expenditure streams are equal in size, the currency exposures will be fully hedged. For example, if a UK company expects to receive $15,000 each month and make monthly payments of the same amount, the income can be used to make the payments, and the net monthly cash flow in sterling will be zero, whatever the exchange rate happens to be.

In practice, foreign currency income and expenditure will not match each other exactly. There will be an excess of income in a foreign currency over payments in that currency, or an excess of expenditure over income. Even so, netting can be used as a **partial hedge**, and the remaining currency exposure is the net difference between income and expenditure.

Netting can also be used to hedge exposures arising from foreign currency-denominated assets and liabilities. For example suppose that a UK bank has loans of €30 million on its books. The loans are assets, and the bank is exposed to the risk of a fall in the value of the euro against sterling. For example, suppose that the sterling-euro rate is £1 = €1.50, and the sterling value of the loan portfolio is £20 million. If the euro fell in value to, say, £1 = €1.60, the value of the portfolio would fall to £18.75 million.

In the same way, if a bank has liabilities in a foreign currency, from obtaining funding in a foreign currency, it will be exposed to the risk of a rise in the value of that currency against its domestic currency.

Netting reduces the risk. To the extent that assets in a foreign currency are matched by liabilities in the same currency, there is no exposure. The remaining exposure is simply the net difference between total assets and total liabilities in the currency. Banks, for example, keep their currency assets (eg loans) at about the same level as their currency liabilities (eg borrowings from other banks or bond issues) in order to contain the currency risk.

5.6 Risk transfer

With risk transfer, a risk is contained or hedged by transferring all or part of it to another person. Commonly-used methods of risk transfer are insurance, forward contracts, securitization and using derivative instruments. Each of these will be considered in turn.

5.7 Insurance

Insurance is a means by which the financial exposure to a risk is transferred legally from one person to another, by means of an insurance policy.

Contractual aspects of insurance

An insurance policy is a contract between the insurer and the insured. The existence of a legally-binding contract depends on consideration being given by both parties. In the case of the insured, consideration is given in the form of the payment of premiums. In the case of the insurer, consideration takes the form of a promise to bear the loss arising from a chance event covered by the contract.

Performance of the contract by the insurer depends on a chance event happening. The insurer is not required to do anything unless that event occurs and the insured suffers a loss as a consequence and seeks to recover the losses by making a claim under the policy. In this respect, insurance contracts are similar to option contracts, which are described later.

An insurance policy is a **contract of indemnity**. The insurer indemnifies the insured against the loss arising on the chance event, and in principle undertakes to restore the insured, physically or financially, to the position that existed before the loss occurred. For example, insurance on the contents of a building indemnify the insured against losses from damage (through fire, flooding and so on), theft and other eventualities. When a loss occurs, the insurer either pays to have the damage restored or the lost item replaced, or compensates the insured financially. There are exceptions to the concept of providing full indemnity. For example, the policy might cover the insured against losses only up to a maximum amount, and any losses in excess of the maximum would be at the risk of the insured. A policy might also provide insufficient cover. For example, if the contents of a building are insured up to a value of £100,000, but the actual total value of the building contents is £200,000, twice as much, the insurer might agree to pay only half of any insured loss that occurs.

In an event of loss, the insurance policy provides for the restoration of the loss to the insured on a replacement cost basis, an actual value basis or an agreed amount basis. When items are insured against loss on a replacement cost basis, the insurer undertakes to replace as new any lost items, or to pay the current replacement cost at the time of the loss. If goods are insured against loss on an actual value basis, the value of any lost items is adjusted downwards from replacement cost, to allow for the age of the item and wear and tear through usage. Many types of insurance policy, such as accident insurance, health insurance and insurance against legal liabilities, provide to indemnify the insured against the actual value of the loss. In the case of legal insurance, the insurer will indemnify the insured against legal costs and damages, and in the case of accident and health insurance, the indemnity is for the actual cost of restoring the insured to a position that existed before the loss occurred. When an item is insured for an agreed amount, the insurer and the insured agree in advance the amount that will be payable in an event of loss or damage. For example, a movie star might have a physical feature insured for a fixed amount.

An insurance policy is also a *contract of utmost good faith*, meaning that the highest standards of honesty are expected from both parties. The insurer is expected to have the ability to pay for the insured's losses, should these occur. The insured person is expected to reveal all the facts relevant to the insurance cover, and should not seek to withhold any relevant information. When facts are withheld, or false information is given by the insured, the insurer will refuse to indemnify the insured in the event of a loss, if the true facts become known.

The structure of an insurance policy

An insurance policy normally contains four elements, three of which are often in standard wording, and common to all policies of a similar type.

- The **declarations** part of the policy is often the only unique part of the policy. It identifies the insured person and the insurer, the nature of the item or assets that are insured, the amount covered by the policy and the premiums payable. Other items unique to the policy, such as its duration and the frequency of premium payments, will also be specified.

- The **insuring agreement** makes up the bulk of the policy. This specifies the losses that are insured.

- An insurance policy will contain certain **conditions** with which the insured must comply, in order to be able to claim for a loss. For example, in the case of home contents insurance, a condition of the policy will be that in the event of a loss, the insured must report the incident to the police and obtain a loss report reference number to quote to the insurer.

- A policy will normally specify **exclusions**. These are circumstances under which a loss will not be insured. For example, insurance of goods in transit against loss or damage will not cover losses arising from acts of war.

Pricing of insurance policies

The insurer is able to finance its exposure to the risks it takes on by pooling risks, and providing insurance cover for similar risks to a large number of different clients. The total premiums receivable from all the policies written by the insurer should be sufficient to cover the losses payable on those policies where claims occur.

An insurance premium has three elements: a loss ratio, an expenses ratio and a profit ratio. The **loss ratio** is the proportion of the total premium that is needed to cover the expected losses for which the insurer will become liable. This part of the premium is based on the insurer's estimate of the average expected loss from the insured risks. For each category of insured risk (eg accident at work insurance, employee liability insurance, medical insurance, car insurance and so on) the estimate of expected losses will be based on industry-wide assessments, but influenced by a statistical analysis of the insurer's own past experience.

The **expenses ratio** in a premium is the proportion of the premium required to cover the insurer's operating and administrative expenses. The **profit ratio** is the percentage of the premium representing the insurer's profit margin.

Suppose that an insurer writes 100 identical insurance policies, for which the annual premium is £1,000 for each policy, and the loss ratio is 85% and the expenses ratio 10%. The average expected loss is £42,500 and the probability of incurring a loss is 2% each year. The insurer would be estimating that the losses it will indemnify in a typical year are £85,000 for all 100 policies taken together (85% of £1,000 x 100 policies, or 2% x 100 policies x £42,500). Its operating expenses will be £10,000 (10% x £1,000 x 100 policies) and the expected profit margin will be £5,000.

Someone taking out insurance cover is exchanging the risk of single large and hard-to-predict losses with the certainty of the regular, small losses incurred by paying the insurance premiums. In the example above, each of the 100 policyholders is exchanging the risk of incurring a large and unexpected loss (in this case a 2% risk each year of a loss that could be £42,500) for the certainty of paying an annual premium of £1,000.

Occasionally, perceptions of risk will change. When the probability of adverse events increases, or when the expected size of losses increases, insurance companies will adjust their policy premiums upwards. For example, in the past when the average size of legal settlements for car accident claims has increased substantially, car insurance premiums have risen sharply. Similarly, following the collapse of US energy corporation Enron in 2001, concerns grew about the potential costs (in the UK as well as the USA) of legal claims against directors and officers of companies for negligence. Insurance companies expressed their opinion that premiums for directors and officers liability (D&O) insurance would have to be increased.

5.8   Credit risk mitigation: collateral and guarantees

Insurance is available for credit risk. A company can buy insurance against the risk that one or more particular debts will not be paid. However, other methods of containing credit risk are more widely used.

Collateral (security)

Banks often demand security (collateral) for loans to customers. When a corporate customer borrows from a bank, the bank normally expects the company to pay the interest and repay the loan principal out of the cash flows from its business operations. Security is a fall-back measure, to be used in an event of default, if the bank then decides that there is no better alternative way of trying to recover the money owed.

If a lender has been given a charge over some or all of the assets of a corporate borrower, as security for the payment of the debt, it is a 'secured creditor' of the company. If the company does not pay the debt on the terms agreed (eg within a certain length of time) the lender can then take steps to obtain payment from the charged assets. It is common practice for a bank to take security for a loan or overdraft, and company debentures might be secured.

The rights of creditors in the event of a liquidation of a company depend on whether the creditor is secured or unsecured (and also on the nature of the security), not on how long the debt is overdue for payment.

'Winding up' occurs when the affairs of a company are brought to an end. The company is put into liquidation, which means that its assets are 'realized' (principally, disposed of through sale), the creditors of the company are paid out of the proceeds and any surplus amounts are returned to the shareholders. Liquidation then leads to the dissolution of the company.

Fixed and floating charges

A charge over assets of a borrower provides a safety net for the lender. If the borrower fails to pay its debt on the terms agreed, the lender can enforce the security, and seek payment from the charged assets. A *company* gives security in the form of either a fixed charge or a floating charge (or both, ie a 'fixed and floating' charge).

A *fixed charge* (or 'specific' charge) over assets of a company, as security for a debt, is a charge attached to a specific asset. If a secured creditor with a fixed charge has to enforce the security in order to get paid, payment will be obtained from the proceeds from selling off the asset. A legal mortgage is a form of fixed charge. By its very nature, a fixed charge is best suited to an asset that the company is likely to retain for a long time, and at the very least until the debt is due to be paid.

A *floating charge* does not attach to specific assets of the corporate borrower as soon as it is created. It is a charge over a class of assets, or possibly more than one class of assets, present and future. A class of assets is all the assets of a particular type, such as all the stock (inventory) of the company, or all the trade debts. The charge is over not just the assets of that class existing at the time the charge is created, but also the future assets of that class that will come into existence in the future, in the normal course of the company's business.

A floating charge might be created over the 'undertaking' or over the 'assets and undertaking' of the company. Here, the charge is over every class of assets of the company, both current assets and fixed assets, present and future.

Where assets are subject to a floating charge, the assets are continually changing. For example, stock is continually used or re-sold, and replaced by new stock. Existing debtors pay what they owe, but the company continues to sell its goods or services on credit, and new debtors are created. Even fixed assets change from time to time, as old plant(s) and machinery (eg office equipment, motor cars etc) are replaced. When a charge over assets is floating, the company is free to deal with the assets, and it does not have to pay the lender from the proceeds from those assets. For example, with a floating charge over the trade debts of a company, the company is not required to use the money collected from its debtors to pay the secured lender. The only requirement is that the company should eventually pay the lender, on whatever terms have been agreed. A floating charge is not enforced unless the corporate borrower defaults under the terms of its loan agreement, for example if it fails to make a payment of interest within a certain time of the due date for payment, or if it fails to make a repayment of loan principal on a due date.

When a floating charge is enforced, the charge **crystallizes** and becomes fixed on the assets (in the charged class) that happen to be there at the time. When a floating charge over the assets and undertaking of the borrower crystallizes, it becomes a fixed charge over all the assets of the company existing at that time.

Collateral (security) and risk containment

Collateral (security) contains the credit risk for a lender, because it provides an alternative source for recovering the debt in an event of default by the borrower. Under insolvency law, a secured lender has prior rights to payment over unsecured lenders, and may seek to recover the unpaid debts from the secured assets. In practice, this can involve the appointment of an administrative receiver to wind up the company and liquidate its assets.

It is by no means certain that the secured assets will be sufficient to repay debts in full, but the prospects for debt recovery are much better for secured lenders than for unsecured lenders and creditors. With loans secured by a first mortgage on commercial property, the prospects for 100% debt recovery should be high, where property values have risen or the property market remains strong.

Guarantees

A guarantee is an undertaking to a lender by a third party. The third party (the **guarantor**) undertakes to pay the unpaid debts of a borrower in an event of default on a loan by the lender to that borrower. Guarantees might be given by one company in a group to a lender to another company in the same group. For example, the parent company of a group might guarantee a loan by a bank to a subsidiary in the group. Guarantees mitigate credit risk, because the lender can fall back on the guarantor as the source of payment if the borrower defaults.

Guarantees can be provided by individuals (personal guarantees) as well as companies.

5.9 Forward contracts (foreign currency and interest rates)

Forward contracts

A forward contract is an agreement 'now' to make a transaction at a time in the future, at a price that is fixed when the agreement is made. By fixing a price now for a transaction in the future, the forward contract reduces the price risk for both buyer and seller. By creating certainty about the price of the future transaction, each has transferred risk to the other.

Forwards contracts are used extensively to hedge exposures to currency risk. An organization might be aware that it will receive a quantity of currency at a future date, which it will want to convert into a different currency. If so, it can arrange a forward foreign exchange contract, fixing the exchange rate for the sale of the currency income in exchange for the second currency. The forward contract will fix the amount of the future income, in the second currency, thereby removing the currency risk.

Similarly, an organization that knows it will have to pay a quantity of a foreign currency at a future date can arrange a forward contract to buy the currency required to make the planned payment. The forward contract, by fixing the cost of the payment, removes the currency risk.

Suppose, for example, that a UK company has agreed to pay $5 million to a US supplier in three months' time. The sterling-dollar exchange rate is currently £1 = $1.40, but the rate has been volatile recently, and the company is worried about the risk of an increase in the value of the dollar against sterling in the next three months. The company can remove the risk by arranging a forward exchange contract to buy $5 million in exchange for sterling in three months' time. The forward rate could be higher or lower than the current spot rate of $1.40, depending on relative three-month interest rates in the UK and the USA. Whatever the forward rate, the contract will fix the amount of sterling required by the company to make the payment to the US supplier. Suppose the forward rate is $1.3950. The cost of the $5 million will be £3,584,229. The company will be required to pay this sterling amount to buy the $5 million in three months, regardless of what the spot sterling-dollar rate happens to be at that time. The spot rate might be above or below $1.3950, which means that $5 million might cost more or less than £3,584,229 in the spot market in three months' time. By fixing the exchange rate in advance, the forward contract protects the company against the downside risk of an adverse movement in the exchange rate (a stronger dollar) but removes the possibility of the upside risk from a favourable movement in the exchange rate (a weaker dollar).

Forward contracts are also arranged on short-term interest rates. These contracts are known as forward rate agreements or FRAs, and are widely used by banks. An FRA can be used to fix an interest rate on a short-term loan or deposit, starting at some time in the future. They can therefore reduce short-term interest-rate risk.

Forward foreign exchange contracts and FRAs are short-term contracts, with a settlement date that is usually several weeks or months ahead. Settlement dates of more than twelve months ahead are relatively uncommon. Although used extensively, they are therefore instruments for managing short-term risk rather than risks over the longer term.

5.10   Securitization

Securitization is an arrangement whereby an organization, known as the **originator**, sells a quantity, a pool or portfolio of its assets or future cash inflows to a **special purpose vehicle (SPV)**. The SPV raises money to pay for the assets or future cash flows by issuing securities to investors. The function of the SPV is to ensure that the assets or future cash flows are put under the legal control of the investors, and could not potentially come under the legal control of the originator or the originator's creditors. The payment of interest on the securities and the redemption of the securities at maturity are paid for out of the cash income from the assets or cash flows that have been sold.

Banks are the originators in most securitization programmes, but the originator could also be a government, a government agency, a non-bank company or other organization. Assets that might be securitized include mortgage loans, credit card debts, commercial loans, leases, student loans and car loans. It is also possible to securitize future income from sources such as intellectual property, government contracts, sports events or even the national lottery. For example, the royalty rights to the early recordings of singer David Bowie were securitized, and the bonds that were issued by the specially-created SPV are known as the Bowie bonds.

Securitization issues might be attractive to investors because they offer an opportunity to invest in certain types of asset, such as residential mortgages, which would not otherwise be possible. Securitization can be attractive to the originator for a number of reasons.

- It is a way of realizing the cash value of assets or future income sooner rather than later. For example, by securitizing a pool of credit card debts, the credit card company is able to obtain cash when the securities are issued, rather than having to wait until the debts are paid by the card holders.

- Securitization takes assets off the balance sheet of the originator, because they are sold to the SPV. This can be desirable for a bank that is unable to increase its lending to customers because it has reached the limit of the lending it can support with its existing capital, under the rules of the Basel Accord on capital adequacy. By selling loans to an SPV, the bank frees up some of its capital and is able to make new loans (replacing the loans that have been sold) without breaching the capital adequacy regulations.

● Selling loans eliminates the credit risk, and selling a future income stream eliminates the business risk (ie the risk that the future income will be less than expected). The SPV buys the assets or future income, and if there are bad debts on the loans, the loss is suffered by the SPV.

An example might help to illustrate the securitization process. Suppose that ABC Bank, which has a large quantity of car loans in its loan book, decides to securitize a pool of three-year loans to a total value of £200 million. The average rate of interest on these loans might be 6%. The bank could set up a separate company, the special purpose vehicle, to buy the loans, and the SPV might issue three-year notes offering interest at, say, 5.5%. The proceeds from issuing the three-year notes would be used to pay for the car loans. The bank will probably enter a service agreement with the SPV to act as its agent for collecting the car loan debts, for which it will be paid a fee. The interest and principal repayments on the loans would be used to pay the interest on the notes and eventually redeem the notes at maturity after three years. Any surplus income for the SPV after paying its note holders will be returned to the bank, under arrangements made when the SPV was first set up.

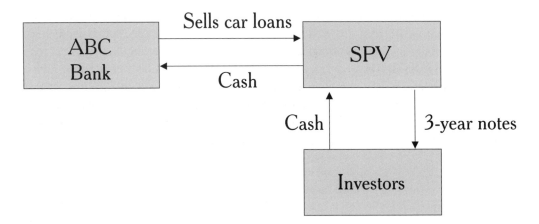

By selling the car loans, the bank receives cash immediately, takes the loans off its balance sheet and transfers the credit risk to the SPV and its investors. The SPV takes on the credit risk, and the bank has no liability to the SPV in the event that the loans provide insufficient income to pay the SPV investors. (However, to protect the SPV investors, the quantity of loans sold to the SPV will usually be sufficient to provide some protection against default risk. This is known as 'over-collateralization'.)

5.11 Introduction to derivatives

A derivative instrument is difficult to define clearly. The original derivatives were transactions in commodities such as wheat, oil and precious metals. Commodities are bought and sold in the 'cash markets'. For example, wheat is sold by farmers and purchased by food producers.

Commodity derivatives are transactions in commodities such as wheat, and are derived from cash market transactions in the commodity. However, they are not the same as cash market transactions.

Financial derivatives are derived from transactions in the 'cash markets' for equities and bonds, and the money markets and foreign exchange markets. These are the markets for buying and selling shares, bonds and currencies, and for borrowing and lending. Financial derivatives are transactions in equities, bonds and currency, and so on, but are not cash market transactions.

During the 1970s, price volatility in the financial markets was associated largely with currency exchange rates. Companies, and banks in particular, recognized the need for tools for managing the enormous risks. The derivatives market was given a huge boost by the development of option pricing theory by the US academics Merton, Black and Scholes. Their work allowed participants in the financial markets to put prices to financial derivatives, and to invent new derivatives to meet the requirements of organizations. The Black-Scholes pricing model remains the basis for option pricing by banks.

Derivatives allow one organization to transfer financial risk to another party that either does not mind taking on the risk or even wants to take on the risk. Suppose for example that a company wants to repatriate its foreign currency income in dollars every three months for the next three years. It can use a currency swap to fix the exchange rate over this time and so remove the risk from a volatile exchange rate for the dollar over that time. Suppose instead that a company's foreign currency income is spread throughout the year and not just realized at fixed dates during the year. This means that the company has a continuing exposure to the exchange rate throughout the year, not just at regular intervals. The currency risk can be hedged with an average price put option (an 'Asian option') that provides protection based on the average exchange rate over the life of the option.

The most common forms of derivative are **swaps**, **futures** and **options**, and they come in different forms. They are used for three purposes: to reduce risk by transferring the risk to someone else, to make profits through arbitrage, and to speculate on favourable movements in market prices.

- **Arbitrage** is the process of making profits from small and temporary price differences that occur in similar but different markets, by buying or selling in each of the markets.

- **Speculation** is the process of risking losses from adverse movements in a price in the hope of making profits from favourable price movements. Derivatives are more appropriate for speculators than buying and selling in the cash markets, because it requires less money to build up a risk exposure in the derivatives market than in the cash market. For example, a speculator in equity price movements might want to build up an exposure to price movements on a portfolio of £100 million of shares. It would cost £100 million to build up this exposure (ie buy the shares) in the cash market for equities. A similar exposure could be built up for a fraction of the cost, using equity index futures or stock index options.

The focus of this text is on risk management, however, and it is this aspect of derivatives that will now be considered.

5.12   Swaps

A swap is an agreement between two parties to exchange (swap) a stream of payments over a specified period of time. There include interest-rate swaps, cross-currency swaps and credit-default swaps.

Interest-rate swaps

A straightforward interest-rate swap (a 'plain vanilla swap') is an agreement between two parties to exchange interest payments on a notional amount of principal. The exchanges occur at regular predetermined intervals over the life of the swap, which might be somewhere between two and ten years. The basis differs for calculating the interest payment for each party. One of the parties pays interest at a predetermined fixed rate throughout the life of the swap. The counterparty (ie the other party) pays interest at a floating rate, which differs from one payment to the next, and is based each time on the current interest level for an agreed benchmark rate, such as the six-month British Bankers Association Libor rate. In the terminology of swaps, one party 'pays the fixed' rate and the other 'receives the fixed' rate.

The interest-rate swaps market is now extremely large, and some banks specialize in acting as swap agreement counterparty. These banks quote fixed rates of interest at which they are willing to enter a swap agreement of a given duration as either the receiver or the payer of the fixed rate. The quoted rate for receiving the fixed rate is higher than the rate for paying the fixed, and the difference in rates provides the bank with a 'turn' or profit margin on its transactions.

The terms of an interest-rate swap might therefore be as follows.

Counterparties:

Payer of the fixed	Bank A
Receiver of the fixed	Customer B
Notional principal	£20 million
Maturity	7 years
Frequency of swap payments	6 months
Payment dates	3 March, 3 September

Interest rates:

Fixed	5.80%
Floating	Six-month BBA Libor rate, as at 1 March or 1 September

For one interest-rate period commencing 3 September, the Libor rate might be, say, 5.50%. The exchange of payments will be made at the end of the interest period, and Bank A will pay a fixed rate of 5.80% on £20 million for the six months, while Customer B will pay interest at 5.50%. In practice, there will be a net payment from A to B for the difference between the two interest amounts.

If, for the following interest period, the Libor rate is, say, 6.25%, Bank A will pay 5.80% and Customer B 6.25%. In practice, there will be a net payment from B to A for the difference between the two amounts.

An exchange of interest payments will occur every six months until the life of the swap ends after seven years.

Interest-rate swaps and risk management

Interest-rate swaps can be used to manage interest-rate risk, and so are particularly useful for organizations such as banks that have large exposures to interest-rate risk. An exposure occurs, for example, when a bank has a quantity of assets earning interest at a floating rate of interest that are financed by liabilities on which payments are at a fixed rate. An interest rate swap can be used to lock in a profit margin on the bank's operations, thereby removing the interest-rate risk. A simplified numerical example will be used to explain this point.

XYZ Bank plans to issue seven-year bonds on which the interest will be 6.50%. It will use the funds to lend to corporate customers at a margin above the Libor rate. As a result of these plans, the bank will borrow at a fixed rate and lend at a floating rate, exposing it to the risk of a fall in the Libor rate at some time over the next seven years. To eliminate this risk, the bank can arrange a swap in which it receives a fixed rate of interest and pays Libor.

The swap should be for a seven-year term. Suppose the fixed-rate in the swap is 6.45%.

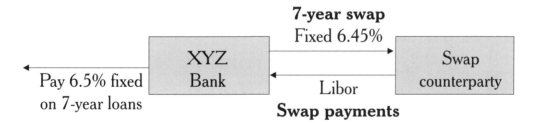

As a result of the swap, the bank has secured funding at a cost of Libor plus 0.05% (5 basis points). If it uses the funds to lend at a floating rate, any interest rate chargeable in excess of Libor plus five basis points will earn a profit for the bank (ignoring the credit risk on the corporate loans). The swap has removed the interest rate risk and increased the likelihood of profits from the lending operations.

Currency swaps

Currency swaps are much less common than interest-rate swaps. They are similar in some respects to interest-rate swaps, but the interest payments are in two currencies. One party pays interest on a notional amount of one currency, and the other party pays interest on an equivalent amount of a second currency. At the end of the swap, there is also an exchange of the currency principal amounts.

Suppose that Bank P and Bank Q arrange a five-year sterling-US dollar currency swap. The current spot rate of exchange is, say, £1 = €1.50, and the agreed amounts of principal are £10 million and $15 million. Interest is payable every six months at a fixed rate, say at 5.5% on the sterling and 4% on the dollars. Bank P might undertake to pay interest at 5.5% on £10 million to Bank Q, which in return pays interest at 4% on $15 million. At the end of the swap, Bank P will pay £10 million to Bank Q and receive $15 million in return.

In the above example, both parties pay interest at a fixed rate. Currency swaps of this type can be used to hedge long-term exposures to currency risk that cannot be hedged by forward foreign exchange contracts. In the example above, the swap allows both parties to fix an effective exchange rate for sterling-dollar over the five-year term of the swap. Swap arrangements can also provide for either or both parties to pay interest at a floating rate: this type of swap can be used to hedge exposures to both currency and interest rate risk.

Credit-default swaps

Credit-default swaps are the most common type of credit derivative instrument, which is a transaction in credit risk. They differ from interest-rate swaps and currency swaps, where both parties make regular payments. In a credit default swap, only one party makes regular payments. In return, the other party agrees to make a payment if a borrower defaults on a debt (a bank loan or a bond issue).

There is a similarity between credit-default swaps and credit insurance. One party to the swap buys credit protection ('sells credit risk') by making regular payments to the other party. These payments are similar to insurance policy premiums. The other party sells credit protection ('buys credit risk'), and is not required to do anything unless there is a **credit event**, such as an event of default by the borrower (the **reference entity**). When a credit event occurs, the swap is terminated. The seller of the credit protection must then make a payment to the other party to cover the loss arising as a consequence of the default.

Credit-default swaps can be used to obtain protection against credit risk in return for the payment of premiums. As such, they are instruments for transferring the risk to another party.

Suppose for example that ABC Bank has lent £10 million to Superglobal plc and there are four years remaining to the end of the loan, when the loan principal will be repaid in full. ABC Bank is now concerned that Superglobal might default, and wishes to buy credit risk protection (sell the credit risk to someone else). It might therefore arrange a credit-default swap with XYZ Bank, a bank specializing in these instruments, for which the terms might be as follows.

Term of swap	Four years
Seller of credit risk (buyer of protection)	ABC Bank
Buyer of credit risk (seller of protection)	XYZ Bank
Reference entity	Superglobal plc
Reference asset	Bank loan by ABC Bank to Superglobal
Calculation amount	£20 million
Annual premium	4% of calculation amount
Premium payable	Annually in arrears

In this example, ABC Bank will pay £800,000 each year to XYZ Bank, either for the full four-year term of the swap or until a credit event occurs, if this happens sooner. If there is no credit event in the four-year period, the swap terminates with ABC Bank having paid £3.2 million in premiums. If a credit event occurs within the four-year period, the swap is terminated and premiums are payable only up to the date of the credit event. XYZ Bank must make a payment to ABC Bank to cover the loss suffered from the default by Superglobal on its loan. For example, suppose that only 25% of the loan is recoverable from the insolvency of Superglobal and liquidation of its assets. The loss will be £15 million (75% of £20 million), and it will be suffered by XYZ Bank rather than ABC Bank.

5.13 Futures

Futures are standardized exchange-traded forward contracts for the buying and selling of an underlying item. They are traded on futures and options exchanges around the world, with each exchange specializing in specific contracts. Many futures are in commodity items, such as wheat, oil, metals and so on, but this text describes financial futures only. With financial futures, the underlying item is something financial – a quantity of shares or bonds, a short-term interest rate (a short-term notional deposit) or a quantity of currency in exchange for another. The UK currently has one exchange trading financial futures, the London Financial Futures and Options Exchange or LIFFE.

Examples of futures

Type	*Example*	*Quantity per contract*
Currency	Dollar-euro	€125,000
Short-term interest rate	Short sterling	Notional three-month deposit of £500,000
	Eurodollar	Notional three-month deposit of $1,000,000
Bond	Long gilt	£100,000 7% UK government bonds
Equity index	FTSE 100	A notional portfolio of shares representing the make-up of the FTSE index, with each index point representing £10. For example, buying FTSE 100 futures at 5100 means buying a notional portfolio of shares worth £51,000.

Futures are instruments for trading in price risk, and can be used to hedge exposures arising from the risk of adverse movements in the price of equities or bonds, or an adverse movement in an exchange rate or a short-term interest rate such as the three-month sterling Libor rate.

● Futures are standardized contracts, and each contract of a particular type is for a standard amount of the underlying item. For example, dollar-sterling currency futures (traded on the Chicago Mercantile Exchange) are each for the purchase or sale of £62,500 in exchange for US dollars. Someone wishing to buy £125,000 in exchange for dollars would have to buy two futures contracts.

● Futures are traded for settlement at specific future dates, with delivery and settlement in March, June, September and December each year. Contracts are therefore bought for a particular delivery date.

● Futures are forward contracts, and the price for the purchase or sale of the underlying item is fixed when the contract is traded.

● A contract is settled at the delivery date in one of two ways, either by physical settlement or by cash settlement. With physical settlement, the seller of the future must deliver the underlying item to the buyer. Bond futures are settled by the delivery of bonds by the buyer to the seller in exchange for a cash payment for the agreed price. Currency futures are settled by an exchange of the currency amounts at the agreed rate. Some contracts are cash-settled, which means that settlement is achieved by means of a cash payment from buyer to seller or seller to buyer, without delivery of the underlying item.

Cash settlement is necessary when the contract has a notional underlying item, such as a notional short-term deposit of funds (short-term interest rate futures) or a notional portfolio of shares (stock index futures).

Someone who opens a position in futures by buying futures contracts is said to take a **long position** in the contract, and someone opening a position by selling futures takes a **short position**. For example, if X buys five December FTSE 100 futures from Y at 5150, and neither of them has an existing position in the futures, X would go long by five contracts in the December futures and Y would go short by the same amount.

A position might be held until the final delivery and settlement date for the contract. In the example above, both X and Y might hold their positions until settlement date in December. Much more commonly, however, positions are closed before final settlement date. A long position is closed by selling an equal number of contracts for the same settlement date, and a short position is closed by buying an equal number of contracts. When a position is closed, a gain or loss is realized on the futures trading, equal to the value of the difference in the buying and selling prices.

Suppose for example that having bought five December FTSE 100 futures at 5150, X decides to close the position on 24 November, and does so by selling five December contracts at 5195. On closing the position, there will be a profit for X of 45 index points per contract (sell at 5195, buy at 5150).

Because futures contracts are all for a standard quantity of the underlying item, each unit of price has a standard value. Here are some examples.

Contract	Price movement	Value
Dollar-euro	$0.0001 per €1	$12.50 (€125,000 x $0.0001)
Short sterling	1 basis point (0.01%)	£12.50 (£500,000 x 0.0001 x 3/12)
Eurodollar	1 basis point	$25 ($1 million x 3/12 x 0.0001)
Long gilt	0.01 (0.01% of face value)	£10 (£100,000 x 0.0001)
FTSE 100	1 index point	£10 per index point

In the example above where X made a profit of 45 index points on closing out his position in five FTSE 100 futures, the total profit on the futures trading would be 45 index points x £10 per point x 5 contracts = £2,250.

Most types of futures contract are priced in the same way as the underlying item. For example, currency futures are priced as an exchange rate and bond futures are priced in the same way as bonds themselves (as a price per 100 nominal value of the bonds, for example at 104.55 or 97.83). An exception is the pricing of short-term interest rate futures, which are priced at 100 minus the interest rate. For example, if the interest rate for a eurodollar future is 5.24%, the price of the future will be 94.76 (100 – 5.24). Similarly, if the interest rate for a short sterling future is 6.85%, the price will be 93.15 (100 – 6.85). This means that when interest rates fall, the price of short-term interest rate futures goes up, and when interest rates fall, the futures price rises.

The exchange as counterparty to all trades in futures

Futures are traded between buyers and sellers on the futures exchange, but when a trade has been made, the exchange steps in to act as a central counterparty. When X arranges to buy futures from Y, the exchange becomes the seller of the contracts to X and the buyer of the contracts from Y. Both X and Y must deal with the exchange as the other party to their transaction. By acting as central counterparty for all trades, the exchange virtually eliminates credit risk for its users (because it is guaranteeing the settlement of all contracts). At the same time, it is able to exert greater control over the performance of contracts by buyers and sellers, as explained below.

The cost of trading in futures

Futures are contracts for trading in the price of a particular item. Trading in futures calls for a lower outlay of cash than trading in the underlying items in the cash market. The initial cost of buying or selling futures is a cash deposit payable to the futures exchange. In the UK, this deposit is called an **initial margin**. The purpose of margin is to cover possible short-term losses on the futures position. For example, if you buy futures and the price subsequently moves against you, the loss you incur in a trading day will be covered by the initial margin you have paid. The exchange will then ask for an additional deposit (known as **variation margin**) to cover possible further short-term losses in the future.

The total cost of buying or selling futures, and so the total cost of investing in futures trading, is the sum of the initial margins payable plus any losses incurred on trading positions (which must be covered by the payment of variation margins).

Futures as a means of hedging exposures to risk

Futures trading can be used to hedge exposures to equity price risk, bond price risk, short-term interest rate risk or currency risk. This can be done by taking a position in futures which is the opposite of the position to be hedged. The aim is to ensure that if an unexpected loss is incurred on the hedged position, there will be a matching gain on the futures position, leaving the net outcome as neither gaining or losing. However, if there is an unexpected gain on the hedged position, there will be an offsetting loss on the futures position, so that the net outcome is neither gain nor loss.

In the following example (slightly simplified), a short-term interest rate exposure is hedged using interest rate futures.

Suppose that in April MNO Bank makes an arrangement with a customer to lend £5 million for three months from 1 September at an agreed rate of 5.75%. It intends to finance the loan by borrowing funds in the London inter-bank market at three-month Libor, from 1 September. The current three-month Libor rate is 5.25%. The bank will therefore expect to make a profit of 0.50% on its three-month lending, amounting (approximately) to £6,250 (£5 million x 3/12 x 0.50%). The bank has an exposure to the risk of an increase in Libor between April and 1 September. If the interest rate goes up, the profit margin on its lending at 5.75% will fall.

Creating a position in short sterling futures can establish a hedge against the interest rate risk. The futures position should provide for an offsetting profit if the interest rate rises. For a profit to occur if the interest rate rises and the price of short-term futures falls, the bank must sell futures. (If the price falls, the bank will close the position by buying futures at a price lower than the original sale price.)

Each short sterling contract is for £500,000. To create a hedge for £5 million from 1 September, the bank must sell ten September contracts, at a price, say, of 94.75 (100 – 5.25). Suppose that Libor rises and on 1 September, the current Libor rate is 5.90%. The futures position should be closed by purchasing ten September contracts. The purchase price might be 94.10 (100 – 5.90). If so the profit on futures trading will have been:

Sell at	94.75
Buy at	94.10
Gain per contract	0.65
Value per basis point	£12.50
Number of contracts	10

Total gain on futures trading = £8,125 (65 basis points x £12.50 x 10 contracts).

The bank will borrow £5 million for three months at 5.90%, to lend at 5.75%, and the loss on lending will be £1,875 (0.15% x £5 million x 3/12). This compares with the profit of £6,250 that was originally envisaged in April. The deterioration in the lending position has been £8,125 (from + £6,250 to - £1,875). However, the unexpected loss on the lending operation has been offset by the gain on the futures hedge.

In this example, the hedge is perfect, and the gain on the futures position has been an exact match for the unexpected loss on lending. It is not usually possible to create a perfect hedge with futures. This is partly because the size of the hedge required cannot be covered by an exact number of futures contracts and partly because the price at which futures are bought and sold does not exactly match the cash market price of the underlying item. In the example above, the September futures price matched the current Libor rate in April when the hedge was created and on 1 September when the position was closed. In reality, there will be some difference between the futures price and the current cash market price.

Nevertheless, futures can be a very convenient method of hedging risks, and they are used extensively by financial institutions such as banks.

5.14   Options

An option is an agreement between two parties, an option buyer and an option seller. An option buyer is often called an option holder, and an option seller is also called an option writer. The purchase cost of an option is called the option premium. An option holder has the right, but not the obligation, either to buy or to sell a specified quantity of a particular item, on or before a specified future date, at a fixed price that is set out in the option agreement. If an option holder exercises his right to buy or sell under the option agreement, the option seller must sell or buy the underlying item at the agreed fixed price.

The option writer receives the premium and is not required to do anything in return unless the option is exercised. The option will only be exercised if it benefits the option holder, and the fixed price in the option is more favourable than the current market price for the underlying item.

Features of options are explained in more detail in the table below.

Underlying item	With financial options, the underlying item might be a quantity of shares in a particular company, a notional portfolio of shares representing an equity index, a notional underlying loan or a quantity of currency.
Right to buy or sell	An option giving the holder the right to buy the underlying item is a **call option**. An option giving the holder the right to sell the underlying item is a **put option**.
Fixed price	The fixed price for buying or selling the underlying item is known as the **exercise price**, exercise rate, **strike price** or strike rate.
Exercise on or before a specified date	An option has an expiry date. If it can be exercised only at the expiry date and not before, it is known as a European-style option. If it can be exercised at anytime up to and including the expiry date and not before, it is known as an American-style option.

Some options are traded on exchanges (for example, options on futures contracts and equity options). Others are traded over-the-counter (for example, interest-rate options).

In-the-money, at-the-money and out-of-the-money options

When an option is first written, its exercise price might be at the same level as the current market price for the underlying item, or it might be higher or lower than the current market price. For example, if someone buys a call option on a company's shares when the share price is 500p, the exercise price could be 500p, higher than 500p or less than 500p. An option whose exercise price is the same as the market price of the underlying item is said to be **at-the-money**. When the exercise price is more favourable for the option holder than the current market price, it is said to be *in-the-money*. A call option is in-the-money when the exercise price is lower than the current market price, because it will be cheaper to exercise the option to buy the underlying item than to buy it in the market. When the exercise price is less favourable for the option holder than the current market price, it is said to be **out-of-the-money**.

Although an option might be in-the-money, at-the-money or out-of-the-money when it is first written, the situation might change in the period up to the expiry date of the option. As the underlying market price changes, an out-of-the-money option might become an in-the-money option, and vice versa. An option will be exercised only if it is in-the-money.

The option premium

Options that are in-the-money obviously have some value to the option holder. However, options that are out-of-the money also have some value up to expiry date, because if the market price of the underlying item changes, the option could become in-the-money. The premium paid for an option represents its value at the time the option is written. However, holders and writers of large quantities of options, such as banks, will monitor the value of their options regularly up to expiry or exercise date, and use option-pricing models to monitor changes in the value of their options.

The option premium, or value of an option, is said to consist of two elements, intrinsic value and time value.

- Intrinsic value is the difference between the option's strike price and the current market value of the underlying item. However, an option has intrinsic value only if it is in-the-money. An out-of-the-money option has zero intrinsic value.

- Time value is a value based on the likelihood that the option will become in-the-money before its expiry date, and by how much. All options have time value, although time value declines as the option approaches expiry. Options that are deeply out-of-the-money have less time value than options that are only slightly out-of-the-money, because they have a lower probability of being in-the-money at the expiry date.

The cost of using options

For an option buyer, the cost of investing in options is the cost of the premiums. An option buyer can therefore take a position in a financial item for the cost of premiums. For example, an investor wishing to take a position in £10 million of shares can do so by purchasing call options on the shares rather than buying the shares themselves. The maximum loss that the option holder will sustain is the premium invested, and this loss will occur when the options are not exercised, but are allowed to lapse at expiry. The potential gain from using options is the benefit from exercising in-the-money options (minus the original cost of the option premium).

A particular advantage of options, compared with forward contracts and futures, is that the option holder is under no obligation to perform the contract when the option is out-of-the-money at expiry. The holder can benefit from the upside risk (ie exercise in-the-money options) and restrict the downside risk to losing the cost of the option premiums. With forward contracts and futures, both parties must perform the contract, so that there is no opportunity for making unexpected gains.

An option writer earns income from the premiums, and does not incur any costs if the options expire out-of-the-money. However, the option writer is exposed to the risk of losses from options being exercised. When options are exercised, the gain for the option holder matches the loss for the option writer.

Options and hedging risks

Financial options are widely used to hedge risk, particularly by financial institutions. If an organization has an exposure to the risk of loss, a position in options can be created (either by buying or selling options) such that there will be a gain on the options position to offset any loss on the hedged position. On the other hand, if there is an unexpected gain on the hedged position, the options will be allowed to lapse, and the unexpected gain will not be offset by any losses on the options position, other than the cost of the option premiums.

An example might help to illustrate options as a hedge. Suppose that a bank trades in foreign currency, and one particular trader specializes in trading in US dollar-yen. The trader might arrange forward contracts to sell dollars and buy yen three months forward, at a rate of 125 yen per dollar, when the spot rate is 124. The forward contracts make the bank long in yen and short in dollars, and so exposed to a rise in the value of the dollar against the yen over the next three months. To hedge the exposure, the bank would need to create a position in derivatives that would give it a profit if the dollar rises in value against the yen, to offset the loss that would occur in its forward contract positions. The bank can use options to create a hedge in either of two ways, although neither approach will create a perfect hedge. The expiry date of the options should coincide with the settlement date for the forward contracts.

- The bank could buy call options on dollars at a rate of, say, 126. If the spot rate for dollar-yen is higher than 126 in three months' time, the bank can exercise its right to buy dollars at 126. It must sell dollars under its forward exchange agreements at 125, so there will be a loss of 1 yen for each dollar sold. However, the call options would limit the maximum loss to one yen per dollar, plus the cost of the option premiums. If the spot rate at expiry is below 126, the options will not be exercised.

- The bank could sell put options at a strike price below 125. If the spot rate for dollar-yen is above 125 when the forward contracts are settled (and the options expire), the bank will incur a loss on its forward exchange contracts, because it would have to sell dollars at 125. However, the put options would not be exercised, and the bank could offset the losses on its forward positions with the income obtained from writing the put options.

5.15 Forward contracts and derivatives as a 'zero sum game'

Spectacular losses from derivatives trading are reported very occasionally. These have been due largely to poor risk management, not to the riskiness of the derivative instruments themselves. A widely-reported case in 1994 was the loss of nearly $200 million by US consumer goods corporation Proctor & Gamble on an interest-rate swap. The swap appears to have been designed to reduce the funding costs for the company if interest rates moved in a particular way, and the swap position was effectively a bet on interest rates rather than a hedge against interest-rate risk.

All derivatives have the quality of being 'zero sum games'. The gains made by one party to the contract are offset by an equal loss for the other party. Take a simple forward exchange contract. Suppose that the spot sterling-dollar exchange rate is £1 = $1.40 and a company makes a forward exchange contract with a bank to sell £2 million forward against the dollar, for settlement in six months, at a rate of $1.41. When settlement date arrives, the spot exchange rate might be higher than $1.41 or below $1.41, but the company must sell £2 million at $1.41 to the bank and the bank must deliver in return the appropriate amount of dollars at this rate. If the spot rate at this time is higher than $1.41 the company will have 'lost', in the sense that it would have earned more in dollars by selling £2 million at the spot rate than at $1.41. The bank has gained an equal amount by purchasing sterling at $1.41 when the spot price is higher. If the spot rate is lower than $1.41 when the forward contract is settled, the company will have gained and the bank lost.

It is unhelpful to think of derivatives and forward contracts in terms of winning and losing. Both parties to a forward exchange contract can use it to take the risk out of their situation. It can be worth reducing risks, even if it means giving up the opportunity for an unexpected gain if spot market prices move favourably. Managing risks by hedging does not mean trying to maximize profits. It means trying to control and contain the risks in such a way as to achieve a satisfactory outcome that balances the return and the risk.

5.16 Risk transfer: a summary

In a text of this size, it is not possible to do more than introduce techniques and instruments for risk transfer. It is important to be aware, however, that these technique and instruments exist, and to understand how they might be used to transfer economic risk to other parties.

Planning risk mitigation strategies

It might seem apparent that since there is a wide range of methods for controlling and containing risk, an organization should plan which methods it should use for each of its risks. In other words, there should be a strategy and policies for risk control and risk containment. When a company has a restricted list of significant risks, formulating policies for risk mitigation might be reasonably straightforward. For example, a company might decide on a policy of hedging currency risk exposures in the forward exchange market, for all exposures above a given size, and the risk-management policy might also specify particular types of risk that must be insured. However, mitigating risk has a cost, and is justified only if the expected benefits exceed those costs.

The complexity and sophistication of risk-management systems tends to increase with the size of the organization, but also varies between different types of business. Banks, more than many other types of business, are expected to have efficient and effective systems for risk management. International banks are either required or expected to comply with regulations for capital adequacy, to ensure that they operate with sufficient capital to sustain their economic risks. These regulations, known as the Basel Accord, are in the process of replacement with a new set of regulations that place even greater emphasis on the importance of risk-management systems.

Risk management in international banks and an outline of the Basel regulations are described in the next chapter.

6

Risk Management in Banks: The Basel Accord

After reading this chapter, you should:

● Understand how international banks apply a common integrated approach to risk management, by requiring banks to maintain a minimum amount of capital to provide cover against the risk of losses

● Understand, in broad outline, the nature of those controls.

Introduction

In 1988, the central banks of the Group of 10 (G10) countries, meeting as the Committee on Banking Supervision at the headquarters of the Bank for International Settlements (BIS) in Basel, Switzerland, produced a set of rules and guidelines for international banks. These rules, known as the Basel Accord, were developed because the central banks believed that the international banking system was operating with far too little capital, due to increasing competition in the banking markets. They felt that banks were trying too chase too much new business with too little capital. The aim of the Basel Accord was to create a 'level playing field' in which international banks could compete, without a significant risk of a financial collapse of one or more banks that might threaten the stability of the entire global banking system.

Although the Basel Accord does not have the force of law, the G10 countries were expected to adopt it and it was hoped that other countries would accept it too, and apply the rules to their banks. This was indeed what happened. Within the European Union, the Basel Accord has been incorporated into EU regulations, currently in the form of the Banking Consolidation Directive and the Capital Adequacy Directive.

The original 1988 Accord focused on the **credit risk exposures** of international banks, and no other risks, and banks were required to maintain a minimum amount of capital (regulatory capital) to cover the risk of losses from those risks. The Accord has been amended several times, most notably in 1996 when a measure was introduced for establishing a minimum amount of regulatory capital for **market risk**, ie risks of losses on trading positions in bonds, equities, foreign exchange, interest rates and commodities.

There are current proposals to replace the 1988 Accord with a New Basel Accord ('Basel

2') which might be implemented during 2005 or 2006. The New Accord will continue to require banks to maintain sufficient capital to cover their risks of loss, and the objective remains to ensure a stable international banking system. A further aim of the New Accord, however, is to provide incentives to banks to develop better risk-management systems and techniques for mitigating risk and pricing risk in their financial transactions, so that the amount of regulatory capital they are required to maintain is more closely aligned to their economic risks.

Whereas the current Basel Accord required banks to maintain a minimum amount of capital to cover credit risk and market risk, the New Accord proposes to introduce a minimum capital requirement for **operational risk**.

This chapter describes the 1988 Accord, and then goes on to consider the changes proposed by the New Accord. An understanding of the rules should provide insights into the nature of risk and risk-management in the banking industry.

6.1   The 1988 Accord

A bank is required to maintain a minimum amount of capital to support its activities, sufficient to cover the credit risk from the assets in its banking book and the market risk from the positions in its trading book. There are different minimum capital rules for items in the banking book and items in the trading book.

Items that are eligible for the trading book include transferable securities such as shares and bonds, money-market instruments, units in unit trusts, futures, FRAs, most types of swap and options on any of these instruments. Assets that are not in the trading book are banking book assets. These include not just loans, but cash and operational assets (such as office equipment). Off balance sheet items (such as guarantees) as well as balance sheet items are included within the definition of 'assets'.

When the Accord was first issued in 1988, the minimum capital rules applied to credit risk only, and no distinction was made between the banking book and the trading book. The minimum capital requirements for market risk were not introduced until the mid-1990s.

Regulatory capital for credit risk

A bank is required to maintain capital equal to at least 8% of the value of its 'risk-weighted assets' in its banking book. For example, if a bank has risk-weighted assets of £1,000 million, it must have capital of not less than £80 million.

The banking book assets are converted into a 'risk-weighted' equivalent. They are grouped into classes and each class has its own risk weighting. Risk weights range from 0% to 100%. For example, a loan to a corporate borrower has a risk weighting of 100%, a loan secured by a mortgage has a risk weighting of 50% and cash has a risk weighting of 0%. The total amount of risk-weighted assets is found by adding up the total of risk-weighted assets for each class of assets.

Banking book assets are classified into five categories or 'buckets', each with a different risk weighting. These include:

Risk weighting	Types of asset
0%	Cash Loans to Zone A central governments/central banks. Zone A countries include all the countries in the Organization for Economic Co-operation and Development (OECD).
20%	Loans to banks in Zone A countries.
50%	Loans secured by a first mortgage on residential property.
100%	Loans to the non-bank private sector, including all loans to companies and individuals. Loans to an AAA-rated corporate therefore has the same risk-weighting as a loan to a small private company or an individual. Loans to banks in 'Zone B' countries with a residual maturity of over one year. Premises, plant, equipment and other fixed assets.

Holdings of government securities could have a risk weighting of 0%, 10% or 20%, depending on national regulations. The risk weighting in these cases is an approximation for market risk.

Risk-weightings are also applied to **off balance sheet items,** such as over-the-counter derivatives (for example, interest-rate swaps and options) and credit guarantees.

Example

ABC Bank plc, a UK bank, has the following assets in its banking book.

	Balance sheet amount	Risk weighting	Risk-weighted assets
	£m		£m
Cash	100	0%	0
Loans to Zone A banks	15,000	20%	3,000
Mortgage loans	2,000	50%	1,000
Loans to companies	15,000	100%	15,000
Loans to individuals	5,000	100%	5,000
Loans to Zone B governments and banks	6,000	100%	6,000
	43,100		30,000

This bank would need capital of at least £2,400 million to cover the credit risk in its banking book.

Other risks in the banking book

Banks are exposed to more than just credit risk in their banking book. For example, they are exposed to foreign exchange risk on their currency lending positions. If they hold securities such as government stock as investments, there will be the risk of a fall in the value of the securities.

In the EU, the Banking Consolidation Directive gives member countries some discretion to build other types of risk into the regulatory capital framework. For example, the 1988 Accord suggests that the risk weighting for investments in government securities should be 0%, 10% or 20%, to reflect market risk in the banking book assets. The UK has chosen a 10% risk weighting for Zone A government paper with a maturity of one year or less and 20% for Zone A government paper with a longer maturity

The UK rules also require regulatory capital to be held to cover minimum currency risk in the banking book and counterparty risk on certain transactions, notably OTC derivatives. (Counterparty is the risk of loses in the event that the other party to the transaction fails to settle its side of the transaction.) Capital requirements for FX risk and counterparty risk in the banking book are calculated in the same way as for the trading book and are described below.

Regulatory capital for market risk

A weakness of the original 1988 Basel Accord was its exclusive focus on minimum capital requirements for credit risk, without any regard to market risk. In the 1990s, the Accord was therefore amended, and a new system was introduced for measuring market risk and requiring banks to maintain a minimum amount of capital to support that risk. The distinction between banking book assets and trading book assets was introduced at this stage.

The minimum capital rules remained the same for banking book assets, but different rules were applied to items in the trading book. For items in the trading book, there must be a minimum amount of capital to cover market risk. Market risk is calculated under six headings:

- **Foreign exchange risk**. This is the risk of losses on trading positions due to adverse exchange rate movements.

- **Equity position risk**. This is the risk of losses on share trading positions due to adverse movements in share prices.

- **Interest rate position risk**. This is the risk of losses on trading positions due to adverse interest rate movements.

- **Counterparty risk or settlement risk**. This is the risk of losses that could arise if a counterparty to a trading transaction fails to settle the transaction.

- **Commodity position risk**. This is the risk for banks trading commodities from adverse movements in commodity prices.

- **Risk from large exposures**. This market risk factor applies only to some banks, and is the additional risk arising from having large exposures on certain market positions. With large exposures, the risk is higher because the impact will be larger if an adverse event occurs.

A bank can calculate the market risk for each of these categories either by applying the standard rules or by using internal risk models, such as a Value-at-risk model. The use of a model is subject to approval by the banking regulator, which in the UK is the Financial Services Authority.

An amount of market risk is calculated for each of the six categories, and the bank is required to maintain at least enough capital to cover the total of the market risk for all the categories. The detailed rules for measuring market risk are not described here.

Problems with the 1988 Accord

The 1988 Accord has achieved much success in bringing financial stability to the international banking system, but there are weaknesses in the rules. The general criticism is measurements of risk under the rules of the Accord are not accurate measurements of the economic risk that the bank really faces. In other words, the rules do not reflect economic reality well enough.

In reality, the credit risk on loans depends on the credit status of the borrower, not on the type of borrower, but the rules of the Accord do not recognize this. For example, the rules assume that the credit risk is the same for a loan to a top-rated international company as it is for a loan to a small business or an individual, and both are given a risk weighting of 100%. A loan to a fairly high-risk bank in an OECD country will have a risk weighting of just 20%, whereas a loan to a top-rated bank in a non-OECD country (such as Singapore) has a risk weighting of 100%.

A further aspect of the 1988 Accord is that there are no minimum capital rules for the operational risks of banks, only for credit risk and market risk.

6.2 Proposals for a New Basel Accord

Proposals have been put forward for a New Basel Accord, to replace the 1988 Accord. The proposals have not yet been finalized, but are expected to be implemented during 2005 or 2006. The overall objective of the New Accord is to encourage banks to maintain sufficient capital that properly reflects the economic risks they face. In the proposals for the New Accord, the Basel Committee commented that: 'Capital requirements that are more in line with risk will allow banks to manage their businesses more efficiently.'

There are three main features that distinguish the proposed New Accord from the existing rules:

- The rules on minimum capital for credit risk in the banking book will be altered, so that the minimum capital requirements reflect economic reality (actual credit risk).

- New rules will be introduced for a minimum capital requirement to cover operational risks.

- The rules on minimum capital should be reinforced by a supervisory regime for banks and greater disclosures by banks about their risks and risk management.

Banks will be encouraged to develop internal models and methods for measuring their risks, with the intention that these models should be used to establish the bank's risks and its minimum capital requirement. However, if a bank does not have an internal model acceptable to the banking supervisor (the FSA in the UK), there are standard rules for measuring risk and capital requirements.

The rules on minimum capital for market risk will remain much the same as under the existing Accord (as amended).

The three pillars of the New Accord

The New Accord will be based on three mutually-reinforcing 'pillars':

- Pillar 1. There will be a minimum capital requirement for each bank, based on an assessment of its credit risk, market risk and operational risk.

- Pillar 2. There should be a supervisory review process, with the banking supervisor assisting banks to develop their risk-management systems and ensuring that the rules are applied properly.

- Pillar 3. Market discipline. The banking market should operate with greater discipline, through greater disclosures by banks.

Changes to the credit-risk weightings

The New Accord will encourage banks to use an internal ratings based approach to measuring credit risk, but a standardized approach will also be available.

The standardized approach

The standardized approach is similar to the approach in the 1988 Accord, except that the risk-weighting rules are different. Risk weightings will apply to credit rating of the borrower rather than the type of borrower.

The proposals include the following risk weightings for corporate loans.

Moody's rating	S & P rating	Risk weighting
Aaa	AAA	20%
Aa	AA	20%
A	A	50%
Baa	BBB	100%
Ba	BB	150%

In the Moody's system of credit ratings, ratings of Baa and above are 'investment grade' credit rating, whereas ratings of Ba and below are non-investment grade (or 'junk' grade). In the Standard & Poor's system, investment grade ratings are BBB and higher.

For credit exposures to sovereign borrowers (governments), where the sovereign is borrowing in a currency other than its own domestic currency, it is proposed to use external credit assessments based on published credit scores of export credit agencies.

The new framework also proposes more *credit risk mitigation*, recognizing that **collateral, netting, credit derivatives** and **securitization** can reduce the risk of loss. Banks will be rewarded for using credit mitigation methods with a lower minimum capital requirement.

The internal risk assessment approach

The New Accord will allow two variants on the internal risk-based assessment approach to measuring credit risk, a foundation and an advanced approach. The calculation of credit risk will be based on an assessment of three factors:

- the probability of default
- the loss in the event of a default
- the exposure at default.

Under the foundation approach, a bank will use its internal model to assess the probability of default and the banking supervisor (FSA) will decide the other factors. Under the advanced approach, the bank will use its internal model to measure all three factors.

The Basel committee has suggested that the internal risk assessment approach should provide a more accurate measurement of credit risk for a bank, and as a result, the minimum capital requirement could be less than if the standardized approach is used.

The internal risk-based method, like the standardized method, rewards banks for the use of credit mitigation techniques. Credit mitigation methods, such as credit derivatives and guarantees, do not always provide a perfect hedge for a credit risk, and there will be some 'residual risk', for which there will be a regulatory capital requirement.

Operational risk

Operational risk is the risk of a direct or indirect loss arising from inadequate or failed internal processes, people and systems, or from external events. It includes legal risks, and risks arising from a breakdown in computer systems. There is an underlying assumption that historical loss data can provide a guide to what future losses might be.

The New Accord proposes three alternative approaches to measuring operational risk:

● a basic indicator approach

● a standardized approach

● an internal measurement approach.

Basic indicator approach

This is the simplest approach. It will be assumed that operational risk can be estimated from a single indicator of the size of the bank's operations. The current proposals suggest that this single indicator should be the bank's gross income, and the operational risk should be estimated as a percentage of gross income. The percentage figure, referred to as the alpha factor, could be about 12%.

The standardized approach

Using the standardized approach, a bank's activities will be divided into different business units, such as banking and investment banking. Each business unit will be subdivided into business activities. For example, banking might be subdivided into retail banking, commercial banking and payments and settlement. A different indicator will be used for each activity, and an appropriate percentage figure applied to each to establish the operational risk for that activity. For commercial banking, for example, the indicator might be the value of the bank's average assets during the year, and a suitable percentage figure (a beta factor) will be applied to this asset value to assess operational risk. Total operational risk will be the sum of the operational risks for each of the bank's business activities.

Internal measurement approach

The internal measurement approach to operational risk will allow banks that have rigorous standards for monitoring and managing their risks to rely on their own internal data to assess the operational risk and minimum capital requirement. The measurement of operational risk will again be dependent on three elements: the size of the exposure, the probability of incurring a loss and the size of the loss if an adverse event were to occur.

> Operational risk = Exposure x Probability of loss x Size of loss, given an adverse event

As with the standard approach, the minimum amount of regulatory capital required is the sum of the regulatory capital needed for each business activity or operation.

At the time of writing, it is still uncertain to what extent banks will be rewarded for **mitigating operational risk** through measures such as **outsourcing of activities** and **insurance**.

Implications of the internal measurement approach for operational risk

For banks that intend to use the internal measurement approach to assessing operational risk, there are some important implications:

- The bank will need a system for monitoring, measuring and reporting operational risk for each business activity and type of operational risk.

- The assumptions used for assessing operational risk should be subject to rigorous testing and verification.

- Banks will need to measure indirect losses from operational risk as well as the risk of direct losses. Indirect losses include the cost of putting something right when it goes wrong, payments to third parties, near misses and write downs. Direct losses will be losses arising directly from an unexpected averse event, such as a computer system breakdown or a terrorist attack on the bank's premises.

- Banks will be required to build up a database of losses over a number of years, and should identify indicators of activity to which the losses appear to be statistically correlated.

To meet these requirements, banks will have to invest more heavily in operational-risk management and risk-management systems. An internal audit department function might be to evaluate the operational risk-management process and the risk-measurement methods.

Supervisory review

The second 'pillar' of the New Accord is supervisory review, which has four underlying principles:

- Banks should have a process for measuring their minimum capital requirement in relation to their risk profile for credit, market and operational risks. They should also have a strategy for maintaining their capital above this minimum requirement.

- The banking supervisor (FSA) should review and evaluate the processes and strategies of the banks for which it is responsible and should check their ability to monitor their compliance with the regulatory capital ratios. The supervisor should take regulatory action if it is not satisfied.

- The banking supervisor should expect banks to operate with capital above the minimum regulatory level, and should have the power to require banks to hold capital in excess of the minimum.

- The supervisor should intervene at an early stage to prevent the capital of a bank from falling below the minimum level, and should require fast corrective action to be taken if the bank's capital is not maintained or restored.

Market discipline

The third pillar of the New Accord is to bolster market discipline by requiring enhanced disclosures of information from banks, for example about the bank's methods for assessing its risk and calculating its minimum capital adequacy. The intention of the Basel Committee is that participants in the financial markets should gain a better understanding of the risk profile of each bank from the information that is made available.

6.3   Conclusion

The existing Basel Accord, and to an even greater extent the proposed New Basel Accord, require banks to monitor and manage their risks. The New Accord should enable banks that manage their risks efficiently to operate with lower minimum capital (or to support a bigger amount of business with their existing capital). This should result in higher returns on capital invested.

It is also likely that the banking supervisor will encourage banks to develop and improve internal systems for monitoring and assessing risks, so that banks will be among the leading organizations for the development of sophisticated risk-management systems.

7

INTRODUCTION TO CORPORATE GOVERNANCE

After reading this chapter, you should:

- Understand what corporate governance is about

- Be able to identify the main stakeholder groups in a company and how these have differing and possibly conflicting interests

- Understand how conflicts of interest might arise between shareholders and directors

- Understand the broad aims of trying to establish 'best practice' in corporate governance.

7.1   The meaning of corporate governance

'Governance' is the act or manner of governing or the function of governing. Corporate governance is therefore the way in which companies are governed. Governance is not the same thing as managing a business and running business operations. It is concerned with exercising overall control, to ensure that the objectives of the company are achieved.

There are differing views about the objectives of corporate governance. From an economic perspective, the aim of a company should be to maximize the wealth of its owners, the shareholders, subject to conforming with the rules of society as embodied in laws and customs. The Organization for Economic Co-operation and Development (OECD), in the introduction to its principles of corporate governance, states that, from a company's perspective, corporate governance is about 'maximizing value subject to meeting the corporation's financial and other legal and contractual obligations'. This inclusive definition stresses the need for boards of directors to balance the interests of shareholders with those of other stakeholders – employees, customers, suppliers, investors, communities – in order to achieve long-term sustained value.'

Another view is that is that aim of corporate governance should be to ensure that the company meets not just the objectives of its shareholders, but also has regard to the interests of other individuals and groups with a 'stake' in the company, and also to the public at large. The OECD recognizes that there is a public policy perspective to corporate governance, as well as a corporate perspective. 'From a public policy perspective, corporate governance is about nurturing enterprise while ensuring accountability in the exercise of power and patronage by

---

firms. The role of public policy is to provide firms with the incentives and discipline to minimize the divergence between private and social returns and to protect the interests of stakeholders.'

Taking a 'stakeholder view', corporate governance is therefore concerned with achieving a balance between economic and social goals and between individual and communal goals. The framework of corporate governance should encourage the efficient use of resources through efficient investment, and also to require accountability from the board of directors for the stewardship of those resources. Within this framework, the aim should be to align, as closely as possible, the interests of individuals, companies and society at large.

No matter whether a corporate view, a stakeholder view or a public perspective view is taken, a broad definition of corporate governance is that it is a structured system for the direction and control of a company, which:

- specifies the distribution of rights and responsibilities between stakeholders, such as the shareholders, the board of directors and management, and

- has established rules and procedures for making decisions about the company's affairs.

Corporate governance provides a structure for setting corporate objectives, achieving those objectives and monitoring progress towards achieving them.

This text focuses on UK listed companies, because good practice in corporate governance has been applied extensively to these by a 'voluntary' code known as the Combined Code.

7.2 Stakeholders in a company

A stakeholder is someone who has an interest. A public company has a number of different stakeholder groups, in addition to its shareholders and the government, and each group has different interests and expectations.

- The **board of directors** is responsible for giving direction to the company and its management, and reserves certain decision-making powers to itself. A board of directors is made up of both **executives** (individuals with executive management responsibilities in the company) and **non-executives** (who contribute to decision-making by the board, but hold no executive management powers). The board has a **chairman**, who could be either a non-executive or alternatively could have some executive responsibilities. There is usually a senior executive director, known as the **chief executive officer (CEO)** or possibly as the managing director. However, when the chairman has executive responsibilities, there will be some 'power sharing' between the chairman and CEO. The primary interest of individual executive directors might be to seek power and authority, together with a high remuneration and a life-style that goes with good pay and conditions.

- **Management** is responsible for running the business and its operations, and is accountable to the board of directors. Individual managers, like directors, might seek to enjoy power, status and good remuneration. The distinction between directors and managers is blurred, because some directors are also executives with senior management responsibilities.

- A company relies on its **employees**, who have their own expectations of what the company should do for them. Since there are usually many employees, their expectations can differ widely. However, most employees expect security of employment, good pay and suitable working conditions. Others might want the company to provide them with training and experience as a path to career progression.

- **Lenders and other creditors** have an indirect interest in a company, but will expect the company to carry on its business with them in an ethical manner, and to pay what it owes. If a company becomes insolvent, and is unable to pay its debts, unpaid creditors might take legal action to obtain control over the business or its assets.

- **Customers** expect a company to provide goods or services of an acceptable quality, to meet a particular need at an acceptable price.

- The **general public**, often with the support of **government**, might consider that it has an important stake in what a company sets out to achieve. For example, commuters might consider transport companies to be under an obligation to provide a reliable service, and households expect utility companies to be under an obligation to provide services such as gas, electricity and water supplies. The public might also believe that there should be severe restraints on what a company should be allowed to do, for example with regard to protecting the environment and preserving the earth's resources.

7.3 Potential conflicts of interest between stakeholder groups

It is unlikely that any company can meet all the expectations of all its stakeholders all of the time. Often, there will be a conflict of interests between different stakeholder groups, with each group wanting different things, in order to achieve incompatible objectives.

From the point of view of corporate governance, the most important potential conflict of interest in a public company is between its owners (the shareholders) and its decision-makers (the board of directors). There is a risk that the directors will control their company in a way that suits their own interests, without due regard to the interests of the other shareholders. When directors run a company in this way, they can often get away with it, partly because they have a better knowledge than the shareholders of what is going on and partly because they are not sufficiently accountable for their decisions and actions.

Shareholders rely on the board of directors to govern their company competently, and monitor company performance and make their decisions to invest in the company's shares, and hold on to them, largely on the basis of information supplied by the directors in the company's name. The value of a shareholder's investment can be at risk from conflicts of interest with the directors, coupled with inadequate information to judge what is happening. The problem has been well expressed by the OECD. 'What makes corporate governance necessary? Put simply, the interests of those who have effective control over a firm can differ from the interests of those who supply the firm with external finance. The problem, commonly referred to as a principal-agent problem, grows out of the separation of ownership and control and of corporate outsiders and insiders. In the absence of the protections that good governance supplies, asymmetries of information and difficulties of monitoring mean that capital providers who lack control over the corporation will find it risky and costly to protect themselves from the opportunistic behaviour of managers and controlling shareholders.'

The relationship between shareholders and the board of directors goes to the heart of many problems with corporate governance, and various elements of 'best practice' are directed towards reducing the potential for conflict, and reconciling as far as possible the interests of the two groups. This key problem will be explored in much more detail in the chapters that follow.

How might conflicts of interest become apparent?

Conflicts of interest might become apparent in a number of different ways. In a most extreme case, it might not become apparent until the company suffers a financial collapse without warning, as in the case of US energy corporation Enron in 2001. Whatever the reasons for an unexpected financial collapse, it cannot be good practice for the directors to be unaware of the impending financial catastrophe, or to be aware of it and fail to inform the shareholders.

In a less extreme form, a conflict of interest might be apparent when directors try to disguise the true financial performance of the company from its shareholders by 'dressing up' the published accounts and giving less-than-honest statements. 'Window-dressed' accounts make it difficult for the shareholders to judge properly the condition of their investment. Concerns about misleading published accounts provided an early impetus in the 1980s and early 1990s to the movement for better corporate governance in the UK.

The directors might reward themselves with huge salaries and other rewards, such as bonuses, a generous pension scheme, share options and other benefits, occasionally extending to the private use of a company luxury yacht or private aeroplanes or helicopters. Institutional shareholders do not object by any means to high remuneration for directors, but consider that rewards should vary according to the performance of the company and the benefits obtained for the shareholders. The main complaint about 'fat cats' directors' remuneration is that when the company does well, the directors are rewarded well, which is fair enough, but when the company does badly, the directors are still paid just as well, which cannot be reasonable. All too often, directors' remuneration has been set without proper regard to the principle of higher reward for better performance to the shareholders' benefit.

Occasionally, decisions by a board of directors appear to be in satisfaction of their own wish for more power and greater rewards, when the shareholders actually suffer loss as a result. A notable example is a high-priced takeover bid. The board of directors of a company might try to acquire another company by making a takeover bid, and raise the offer price to a very high level in order to obtain the acceptance of the bid by the target company shareholders. A successful takeover will increase the size of the business empire run by the board of directors, and they might well pay themselves more for the extra responsibilities and status they have acquired. However, if the price paid for the target company was too high, the 'winners' will be the target company shareholders who were paid an excessive price, and the loss will be borne by the shareholders of the 'successful' bidder. (This loss will probably become evident in the form of an eventual fall in the company's share price.)

A more subtle potential conflict of interest is risk awareness. When investors buy shares in a company, they have an idea of the type of company it is, the nature of its business, the sort of returns it is likely to pay and the nature of its business risks and financial risks. To shareholders, both return and investment risk are important. The directors, on the other hand, are rewarded on the basis of profits or dividend growth (returns), but are not necessarily concerned too much about the risk aspects of their business. An awareness of risk, and the need to monitor and manage risk, has now become an important element of corporate governance best practice in the UK.

7.3   Corporate governance and risk management

Issues of risk management and corporate governance are closely connected. Interest in matters of corporate governance has grown over the last ten years or so, with the development of principles for corporate governance and codes of best practice.

The impetus for change began with a number of spectacular and well-publicized corporate failures. In the USA, many companies in the savings and thrift industry had to be rescued from financial collapse in the 1980s. In the UK, investors suffered in the 1980s and 1990s from the collapse of companies such as Polly Peck International, the Bank of Credit and Commerce International, British and Commonwealth, Robert Maxwell's Mirror Group News International, Barings Bank and others. In some cases, 'creative accounting' and inadequate financial regulation were seen as a cause of the corporate failure. In others, such as the collapse of Barings Bank due to the losses of a rogue trader, inadequate controls were a key factor. In the USA, the collapse of Enron in 2001 was unexpected because the markets had no ideas of the precarious financial position of the company, and the quality of its financial reporting and auditing were called into question and blamed for the losses suffered by investors.

Obvious questions are asked when a company collapses unexpectedly. Why did it happen? What should have been done to prevent it? What should be done to reduce the risk of it happening again? The reasons are often incompetence, fraud or abuse. Inevitably when a company fails, doubts are raised about the management, and criticisms voiced that the shareholders lost their investment because of careless or unscrupulous – or even dishonest – senior management. There could be a suspicion that the company was being run for the benefit of the all-powerful chairman-cum-chief executive, with little concern for the interests of the shareholders. The history of Robert Maxwell is a notorious example.

Poor corporate governance does not necessarily lead to financial collapse, but it will often result eventually in a falling share price and severe losses for shareholders. Companies with a strategy of growth through acquisition are an example. The board of directors of an acquisitive company can sometimes be accused of destroying shareholder value by overpaying for the purchase of target businesses. A policy of growth by acquisition to build up a large commercial empire, without proper consideration being given to the financial consequences, will eventually result in a falling share price. For example, in 2002 it was revealed that the board of US conglomerate Tyco, reported to be in financial difficulties and with a share price that had halved over a short period of time, had spent $8 billion in the previous three years buying up about 700 companies. Because the size of each of these acquisitions was 'immaterial', none of them had been announced to the markets or approved by the shareholders.

It has been observed that a common denominator in past corporate failures has been a lack of effective control over the company, and the absence of effective risk management. The main problem is normally not so much dishonest directors, but a well-intentioned board of directors failing to carry out its duties adequately. These duties must include ensuring that an effective system of risk management is in place. Investors want the reassurance that their company is aware of the risks it faces, and that a system for monitoring and controlling them is in place. Risk management itself is therefore an element of corporate governance.

7.4   Information and accountability

There is growing pressure on companies from institutional investors (fund managers) for the board of directors to be more accountable to the shareholders. Institutional investors are the major shareholders in UK public companies, and expect their voices to be heard, particularly when they regard themselves as long-term investors in the company rather than short-term buyers trading in shares for a quick profit. Investment is now global. US investment institutions (the largest investors in the world) buying shares in foreign markets expect the same corporate governance practices as they are used to in the USA. When they do not find it, they demand change. Much of the pressure for improvements in corporate governance in countries such as Germany, France, Italy and the Netherlands, has come from US and UK institutions.

Companies cannot ignore investors' concerns if they expect to raise new capital. Sound corporate governance is necessary to create confidence in the financial markets. To attract new funding, companies need to demonstrate to potential investors, both nationals and foreign investors, that they are being managed responsibly and prudently. A key element in a system of sound corporate governance is therefore **disclosure of information**. Openness provides a basis for confidence.

In addition to providing adequate disclosures to shareholders, directors should also be **accountable**. Another element in corporate governance is the way in which the performance of the directors is monitored and judged. According to financial theory, the objective of a company should be to maximise the wealth of its shareholders. This is achieved by maximizing the financial return to the shareholder through increases in the value of the shares plus the dividends paid out of profits. It ought to follow that directors could be held accountable to shareholders on the basis of the returns that the company has achieved.

However, there is no agreed rule for deciding the time period over which the returns to shareholders and increases in their wealth should be measured. Should the success of a company in meeting its overall objectives be measured over a period of one year, two years, five years, ten years or even longer? The tendency in practice is to take a short-term view and judge the share price and dividend performance over each twelve-month period. However, in the short term, a company's share price might rise excessively high or fall to unrealistically low levels due to the state of the stock market. In the longer term, the value of a share should relate to the ability of the company to earn profits or cash flow, but this is not necessarily so in the short run. The existing share price might be unsustainable in view of the company's underlying profits, and will eventually fall or rise. Short-term performance is not an adequate gauge for the long term.

When company performance is judged by the return to shareholders over a 12-month period, there is a risk that the directors of the company will focus on short-term results and daily movements in stock market prices. They should really be looking after the underlying business of the company and its profitability over the longer term.

In an article in the *Financial Times* (29 January 2002) John Kay, reflecting on the reasons given by the former finance director of Marconi for the company's financial collapse in 2000, made the following comment. '[A director's] job is to run a business that adds value by means of the services it provides to customers. If he succeeds, it will generate returns to investors in the long term. And this is the only mechanism that can generate returns to investors. The problem is that the equivalence between value added in operations and stock market returns holds in the long run but not the short. Share prices may, for a time, become divorced from the fundamental value of a business. This has been true of most share prices in recent years… In these conditions, attention to total shareholder returns distracts executives from their real function of managing businesses.'

7.5 Achieving best practice

The broad issues in corporate governance could be summarized as follows:

- The objectives of a company need to be understood. In economic theory, the main objective is to maximize shareholder wealth, but there are other stakeholder groups whose interests cannot be ignored.

- The individuals who have the powers to control a company need not be the owners. Conflicts of interest can arise between different stakeholder groups, and in particular between the board of directors and the shareholders, where these are different individuals.

- Those individuals with power to control a company should have clearly-defined responsibilities.

- When a company collapses, shareholders, employees, creditors, customers and the public all suffer loss, but the cause of the collapse can often be attributed to incompetence or abuse by the directors and management.

- 'Best practice' in corporate governance can provide a risk-control framework, to limit the possibility of corporate failure and improve the likelihood of the company's achieving its objectives.

- Best practice involves disclosure of information, and accountability of those in power.

Company law provides some rules on corporate governance, which are probably sufficient for many small private companies, where the owners are also its directors and managers, so there are no conflicts of interest. The problems and conflicts are greatest in public companies where there are many shareholders and the directors are either small shareholders themselves or do not hold any shares at all, and company law does not provide sufficiently robust rules to ensure good corporate governance. Self-regulatory systems for corporate governance have therefore been developed for stock market companies, most notably in the USA and the UK.

The legal aspects of corporate governance are described in Chapters 8 and 9. The self-regulatory framework for stock market companies and other elements of corporate governance will be explored further in Chapters 10 and 11.

8

BACKGROUND COMPANY LAW

After reading this chapter you should:

- Understand the nature of corporate personality and the legal status of a company

- Understand the purpose and contents of a memorandum of association and articles of association

- Have an understanding of the powers of shareholders and directors under company law in England and Wales and the articles of association

- Have an understanding of the rights of shareholders under company law in England and Wales

- Understand the rights of shareholders and powers of directors with regard to the issue of new shares

- Understand the purpose of the UK Listing Rules and their relevance to corporate governance

- Explain the concept of capital maintenance.

8.1   Companies and corporations

In the UK, there are three types of 'body corporate' or corporation: a corporation formed by the grant of a royal charter from the Crown, a statutory company created by Act of Parliament, and a company formed by registration under the Companies Act 1985. The first two types of corporation are uncommon, and the normal method of incorporating a business is by registration under the Companies Act.

A partnership might include the word 'company' in its business name, such as 'H Jones & Company'. However, a partnership company of this type is an unincorporated association of its members, and is not a company in the legal sense.

The most important piece of legislation in England and Wales dealing specifically with companies is currently the Companies Act 1985, but this has been amended by various items of legislation, notably the Insolvency Act 1986 and the Companies Act 1989.

A registered company is formed through a process of incorporation and is registered at the Companies Registry. The Registrar of Companies, the Department of Trade and Industry (of which the department of the Registrar is a part) and the courts all have powers of regulation and investigation. The public has the right to access certain records of a company, copies of which are held at the Registry. Unincorporated businesses are subject to much less regulation and supervision.

8.2 Corporate personality and legal status

A company is owned by its members (the shareholders) and is managed by its directors. However, as a corporate body, it has its own legal identity. It exists as a separate legal personality, distinct from its owners and managers. Even when a company is 100% owned by one person, it is a separate legal personality from the owner.

The significance of legal personality is that a company is subject to the same general law that applies to individuals, unless express provision is made otherwise by legislation. In particular, a company can enter into contracts in its own name, and is subject to the law of contract. Companies can therefore own property, borrow money and employ individuals.

This separate legal status of a company, distinct from its owners, is referred to as the 'veil of incorporation'.

The consequences of having a separate legal personality

A company has certain distinct characteristics arising from its separate legal personality. One of these is **limited liability**, which is explained later. Other characteristics are as follows.

- The interest of a member in a company is a form of property. In most companies, ownership in a company is measured by shares, and the members are shareholders. A shareholder can transfer his or her share of the ownership of the company by transferring shares to another person, subject to any restrictions on share transfers that might be imposed by the company's constitution (articles of association). A change in the membership of a company through a transfer of shares has no effect on the company itself, because its legal status and corporate identity are unaffected by the change.

- A company owns its own assets and rights, and has its own liabilities. Debts of the company are not the debts of the company's owners. Similarly, assets of a company legally belong to the company, and not to its owners.

- Sums paid by the members of a company to acquire their shares form the capital of the company. If it is a company with limited liability, it cannot distribute any of this capital back to its members (unless the company is wound up), but must retain the capital as a fund to meet its own debts.

- A company is an artificial person and cannot manage itself, and must therefore have individuals to run it. The management of a company is entrusted to its directors. Together with the company secretary, the directors are the **officers** of the company, who are subject to a range of statutory and non-statutory rules and regulations designed to ensure that they do not abuse their position of authority.

8.3   Types of company

Limited and unlimited liability: share capital

A registered company may be a company limited by shares, a company limited by guarantee or an unlimited company.

Most registered companies are **companies limited by shares**. A company issues shares with a nominal or face value, and shares are issued in one or more different classes. Typically, there is one class of ordinary shares, but in some companies there are two or more classes of ordinary shares (known perhaps as 'A' ordinaries and 'B' ordinaries). There could also be one or more classes of preference shares. The issue price of new shares, which is the price paid by investors to acquire them, is often higher than the nominal value. However, regardless of the issue price paid, each share in the same class carries the same rights (for example, rights to dividends, voting rights and rights in a liquidation) as every other share in the same class.

For example, DEF Limited might issue 200 shares with a nominal value of 50p each when it is first incorporated, with D buying 100 shares for £2 each and E buying the other 100 shares for £2.50 each. The company might then issue a further 100 shares that are bought by F for £4 each. The issued share capital of DEF would be 300 shares of 50p each, with D, E and F each holding an equal (one-third) share in the ownership of the company.

The word 'limited' refers to the liabilities of the owners (shareholders) for the unpaid debts of the company. A limited company, as a legal person, is fully liable for the debts it incurs. Should it be unable to pay its debts, the liability of its shareholders is limited to the capital they have already invested. In accounting terms, this is the share capital and balance sheet reserves of the company.

Very occasionally, shares are 'partly paid' rather than 'fully paid'. When shares are issued partly paid, the shareholders are required to pay a proportion of the price of the shares to begin with, and the balance at a later date. For example, a company might issue new shares of £1 partly paid, with the initial payment restricted to 75p. The balance of the price will be payable later. If a company has partly paid shares when it goes into liquidation, the shareholders will also be liable for the unpaid amount on the partly paid shares. However, partly paid shares are rare in the UK.

Limited liability can be illustrated with a simple example. Suppose that ABC Limited has share capital of £200,000 and balance sheet reserves of £50,000. Total shareholder capital is therefore £250,000. If, for some reason, the company is unable to pay its debts and is forced into liquidation, the maximum liability of the shareholders is the £250,000 investment represented by the share capital and reserves. This has already been invested in the company, and the shareholders will not be required to make further payments to settle the company's unpaid debts. At worst, they will get nothing back when the company is broken up and its assets sold off to pay off as many of the unpaid debts as possible.

In this respect, the owners of a company are in a different position from partners in a normal partnership (although not a limited liability partnership). If a partnership business is unable to pay its debts, each individual partner, together with the other partners as individuals, is 'jointly and severally liable' for the unpaid debts of the business. Partners could stand to lose, not only their investment in the business, but also their privately-owned assets.

Companies limited by guarantee are companies in which the liability of each member is limited to a specified amount that he has undertaken to contribute towards the unpaid debts, in the event of the company is wound up. Most companies limited by guarantee are non-trading companies, such as charities.

In an **unlimited company**, the liability of the members is unlimited, in the event of the company being unable to pay its debts. If the company goes into liquidation, the members are liable for all the unpaid debts, and will be required to pay out of their private assets. Unpaid creditors cannot sue the members individually, but must make a claim for payment in the company liquidation process, and the liquidator will call for contributions from individual members.

Public and private companies

A company limited by shares is either a public company or a private company. A company is a public company if its constitution (memorandum of association) states that it is, and if the necessary procedures have been carried out to register the company as a public company. A private company is defined in a negative way: it is a company that is not a public company.

Public limited companies (PLCs) come into existence in either of two ways. In some cases, a company might be incorporated as a public company. Alternatively, a private company might re-register as a public company.

In many respects, public companies and private companies are subject to the same regulations. The main differences are summarized below.

Name	The name of a public company must end with the words 'public limited company' or its equivalent (such as 'plc'). The name of a private company must normally end with the word 'Limited'. For Welsh companies, Welsh language equivalent names can be used.
Issuing shares to the public	A public company can issue shares and debentures to the general public. A private company is prohibited from doing so.

Minimum number of members/shareholders	A public company must be a company limited by share capital, and must have a minimum number of two shareholders. A private company can be formed by just one person. In practice, public companies often have many shareholders among the investing public, whereas many private companies are owed by one person.
Minimum share capital for companies limited by shares	A public company cannot start to trade until it has been issued with a trading certificate by the Registrar of Companies. A trading certificate is dependent on the Registrar being satisfied that the company has allotted (issued) at least the 'authorized minimum' amount of shares. The authorized minimum is currently £50,000 (nominal value). There is no minimum share requirement for private companies.
Minimum number of directors	Every public company (registered on or after 1 November 1929) must have at least two directors. A private company must have at least one director.

Typically, a public company is a large company with shares owned by a large number of investors. A private company is often either a small independent company in which the owners are also the directors, or a subsidiary company that is 100% owned by a 'holding' company or 'parent' company. However, not all companies conform to these stereotypes. Some private companies are very large. Many PLCs are quite small, and could be owned by a small number of shareholders. A PLC might even be 100% owned by a parent company.

Other categories of company

Two other methods of categorizing companies are worth noting.

Companies are either **quoted** or **unquoted**. A quoted company is one whose shares are traded on a stock exchange, such as the London Stock Exchange, and its prices are therefore quoted on the exchange. A quoted company must be a public limited company (but a public limited company does not have to be a quoted company). Some quoted companies are referred to as **listed companies**. A listed company is a quoted company whose shares have been admitted to the Official List and are traded on the main London Stock Exchange. The Official List is explained later.

The Companies Act 1985 provides for many private companies to be categorized as **small** or **medium-sized**. Small companies are allowed to provide much less financial information than large companies in the annual accounts they file with the Registrar of Companies.

Medium-sized companies are also exempted from filing certain financial information, but the exemptions are fewer than for small companies.

8.4   Written constitution

Being an artificial person, a company cannot have a mind of its own and it is therefore necessary to establish the way it is established and governed, and the rights and duties of its members and officers (shareholders and directors). A company is therefore required by law to have a written constitution, in the form of a **memorandum of association** and **articles of association**.

The memorandum sets out certain matters required by the Companies Act.

The articles consist mainly of rules for the internal governance of the company.

8.5   Memorandum of association

The legal requirements as to what the memorandum of association should contain vary according to the type of company. A summary is given in the table below.

	Private co, limited by shares	Private co, limited by guarantee	Public company	Unlimited company
Company name	Yes	Yes	Yes	Yes
Statement that the company is a public company			Yes	
Country of location of registered office (England and Wales, Scotland or Wales)	Yes	Yes	Yes	Yes
A statement that the liability of the company's members is limited	Yes	Yes	Yes	
Amount of authorized share capital	Yes		Yes	
Statement of the amount each member will contribute in a winding up		Yes		

Authorized share capital

The authorized share capital is the maximum amount of shares that the company is currently permitted to issue. The share capital must be divided into a number of shares of a specified nominal value. For example, if the authorized share capital is two million shares of £1 each, the company can issue up to this maximum number of shares without the need to alter its constitution.

If a company wants to issue new shares so that the total number of issued shares would exceed the authorized maximum, it will be necessary first of all to gain shareholder approval for a change in the memorandum, to increase the authorized share capital.

For example, suppose that a company has authorized share capital of 600,000 shares of £1, and has already issued 500,000 shares. Suppose that its directors now want to issue a further 250,000 shares. To do this, the company must first increase its authorized share capital to at least 750,000 shares. The directors might propose a higher new limit, to give them scope to issue more new shares later. The approval of the shareholders will be required to amend this item in the memorandum, by means of an ordinary resolution in a general meeting of the company.

Objects clause

The objects clause in the memorandum sets out the aims and purposes of the company. A transaction by the company outside the scope of its objects is *ultra vires* (beyond its powers) and so, in principle at least, is unenforceable. For example, if a company's objects clause states that the purpose of the company is retailing, the company would be acting *ultra vires* if it diversified into, say, aircraft manufacture.

In practice, however, the Companies Act 1989 diminished the significance of the objects clause and the risk of a company acting *ultra vires*. A company may now include in its objects clause a statement that its object (or one if its objects) is to carry on business as a 'general commercial company'. This allows the company to carry on any trade or business whatsoever, and the company has the power to do anything conducive or incidental to carrying on any business or trade.

The directors of a company have a duty to observe any limitation on their powers arising from the objects clause in the company's memorandum. For a director to do anything outside the objects of the company would be an abuse of his or her powers, and the director could be liable for any losses incurred as a consequence. Any *ultra vires* action by a director would have to be ratified by the shareholders (by means of a special resolution at a general meeting of the company).

8.6   Articles of association

A company must have articles of association, which are a form of contract between the company and its members (shareholders). These deal mainly with the conduct of the company's affairs. When a company is first incorporated and applies for registration, it must deliver a copy of its articles to the Registrar of Companies.

The articles can be written from scratch. It is easier, however, for a company to adopt a standard set of articles provided in the Companies Act, with perhaps a few modifications to suit its particular requirements. The standard articles appropriate to a company limited share capital are known as the Table A articles, and if a company does not have any articles of its own, the Table A articles will apply.

The Table A articles consist of 118 paragraphs, which include the company's constitutional rules relating to:

- Share capital and share certificates.

- The transfer of shares, and purchases by the company of its own shares.

- Alterations of share capital.

- General meetings of the company: the right of shareholders to attend general meetings, giving notice of meetings, procedures of meetings and voting rights of shareholders.

- Directors: the number of directors, their powers, their appointment and retirement, disqualification, remuneration and proceedings.

- The company secretary and minutes of meetings of the company.

- The power of the company to declare a dividend, and the rights of shareholders to receive dividends.

A company can alter its articles by a special resolution of the shareholders in a general meeting.

8.7   The powers of shareholders and directors

Although a company is a legal entity, it cannot take decisions itself. Decisions are taken either by the shareholders or the directors.

It might be helpful to remember who the shareholders and directors are in different types of company. The problem of who has the power, the shareholders or the directors, is only significant when they are two separate groups.

- In many small private companies, the major shareholders are also the directors of the company.

- When a subsidiary company is wholly-owned by a 'parent company' or 'holding company', the directors will be appointed by the board of the holding company, and a holding company director might sit on the board of the subsidiary.

- In most large quoted public companies, there are many small investors (both 'retail' investors as well as 'institutional' investors such as pension funds and unit trusts) with no individual shareholder having a controlling interest. The directors might also be shareholders, but need not be. In large companies, the potential for a conflict of interests between directors and shareholders can be very high.

The powers of shareholders

The powers of shareholders to make certain decisions for the company are granted either by law or by the company's articles of association. These powers, however, are limited to a fairly small number of decisions, such as the power to:

- Alter items in the company's memorandum of association, such as the company's name, its objects clause and the authorized share capital.

- Alter the articles of association.

- Change the status of the company, from private company to public company, or from public company to private company status.

- Remove a director from office (rare in practice) and reappoint directors standing for re-election (normally a routine procedure at the annual general meeting).

- Approve the proposed final dividend at the annual general meeting, or vote to reduce the proposed dividend.

- Reappoint the company auditors.

- Wind up the company voluntarily.

Decisions by shareholders are taken by votes at a general meeting of the company, which is either the annual general meeting or an extraordinary general meeting. Normally, only ordinary shareholders may attend general meetings. Where the company has more than one class of shares, it might very occasionally be necessary to call a meeting of a particular class of shareholders other than the ordinary shareholders (for example a class meeting of preference shareholders).

Votes are taken on resolutions that are notified in advance of the meeting. Some decisions require an ordinary resolution and others a special resolution. An ordinary resolution is carried by a simple majority of over 50% of the votes cast. A special resolution requires at least 75% of the votes cast to be carried. (There are also extraordinary resolutions, requiring 75% of the votes cast, but these are unusual.)

Shareholders can vote by attending the meeting in person or by appointing another person (a 'proxy') to attend and vote on his or her behalf. Alternatively, a shareholder can vote by proxy by post. This involves returning a preprinted form or card to the company. This proxy voting card shows each of the resolutions to be voted on at the meeting, and the shareholder indicates how he or she wishes to vote, for or against, on each resolution and also indicates the person who should cast the proxy votes on his or her behalf. (This could be the chairman of the board.)

To speed up proceedings for passing non-controversial resolutions, an initial vote is usually taken on a resolution by a show of hands of the members present, with proxies not permitted to vote. Each member has one vote, regardless of the number of shares owned. However, a poll can be demanded for any resolution. In a poll, the votes are counted for all the persons present at the meeting, including proxy votes, and shareholders (or proxies) have one vote for each share they own (or represent). This means that in a poll, the vote of a shareholder with 10,000 shares carries ten times the weight of a vote by a shareholder with 1,000 shares.

The powers of directors

The powers of shareholders to make decisions for the company are restricted, and most powers to make decisions and take action are given to the directors.

Article 70 of Table A permits the directors to exercise all the powers of the company, subject only to the provisions of the Companies Act, the company's memorandum and articles of association, and any directions given to the directors by a special resolution of the shareholders in general meeting.

Powers are conferred on the directors collectively, with decisions taken at board meetings where a quorum is present. However, a requirement for all decisions to be taken at board meetings could be inefficient, and the Table A articles provide for the collective powers of the directors to be delegated to individual directors or committees of the board. The board may also appoint a managing director and executive directors.

In principle, the actions of directors are restricted by the company's memorandum and articles. The Table A articles include a requirement that at every annual general meeting, one-third of the directors should retire and offer themselves for re-election, by ordinary resolution of the shareholders. Shareholders also have the power to remove a director from office. In practice, however, shareholders are not able to enforce their powers easily in the absence of a single dominant shareholder.

However, when there is a dominant shareholder with enough shares to remove directors from office, ie a controlling interest in the company, the shareholder will be able to dictate decisions by the board of directors.

8.8   Rights of shareholders

A distinction can be made between the rights of shareholders and their powers to make decisions for the company.

Shareholders are granted certain rights by the Companies Act and by the articles of association, to protect them against unfair treatment by the directors. Important rights are summarized as follows:

●   A right of the shareholders to an annual general meeting of the company.

●   A right of each shareholder to receive advance notice from the company of a general meeting.

- A right of each shareholder to vote at general meetings, either in person or by proxy.

- A right of shareholders to inspect the minutes of general meetings.

- A right to have the shareholder's name entered in the company's register of members.

- A right to a share certificate (although virtually all public companies also offer the option of holding shares in uncertificated electronic form).

- A right to receive a copy of the company's annual report and accounts.

- A right to receive a dividend, when the company pays a dividend to other shareholders of the same class.

- A right to transfer shares to another person, by sale or gift, subject to any restrictions on transfers imposed by the company's articles of association.

The protection of minority shareholders and minority rights

A minority shareholder is a shareholder who does not have a sufficient number of shares to affect decisions taken by the company in general meeting, nor to influence the decisions of the directors. Even as a group, minority shareholders are therefore relatively powerless against the directors of the company, or against a controlling shareholders or a majority group of shareholders.

Some rights are given to minority shareholders by company law, to give them a small degree of protection against adverse decisions by the directors or the majority of shareholders.

- Shareholders representing at least 5% of the total voting rights have the right to place a resolution on the agenda for a general meeting of the company and to circulate a written statement to the other members about any resolution that will be proposed at the next general meeting.

- Shareholders representing at least 10% of the company's shares can exercise a right to call an extraordinary general meeting.

- Shareholders representing more than 25% of the voting rights can defeat a special resolution at a general meeting.

- Any member individually can petition the court for an order on the grounds that the company's affairs are being conducted in a way that is prejudicial to the interests of the shareholders generally or to a group of its shareholders.

(Note: Minority interests also have certain rights under the Takeover Code, which tries to ensure fair treatment for all shareholders in the event of a takeover or merger.)

8.9   The issue of new shares

The need for regulation of new issues

A variety of rules and regulations apply to the issue of new securities by a company, and in particular the issue of new shares. This is a matter of some relevance to corporate governance, because the issue of new shares could affect the rights of existing shareholders.

A simple example might illustrate this point. Suppose that a company has 100,000 shares in issue, of which 60,000 shares are held by a group of investors supporting the board of directors, and 40,000 shares are held by a group opposing the board of directors. The board of directors would like to obtain shareholder approval to a scheme that requires a special resolution (75% of the vote in favour). Unless there are regulations to prevent them, the directors could decide to issue 60,000 new shares, bringing the total up to 160,000 shares, and allot all the new shares to their supporters. The group supporting the directors would then have 120,000 out of the 160,000 shares in issue, sufficient to carry a special resolution.

The key point this example illustrates is that the rights of shareholders could be adversely affected if the directors have unrestricted powers to issue new shares and freedom of choice in deciding to whom the shares should be allotted. In an extreme case, without regulation, the directors would be able to issue shares to a single investor so as to give the investor a controlling interest in the company.

Power of directors to allot shares

Section 80 of the Companies Act 1985 gives the board of directors power to allot new shares up to a specified limit. This limit is normally set by the shareholders, by means of an ordinary resolution at a general meeting of the company. The directors' powers of allotment must have an expiry date as well as a maximum limit. The authority of the directors to allot shares can be renewed when their existing permission expires, but in the case of a public company, the renewal period cannot exceed five years. The powers given to the directors could therefore be perpetual, but subject to periodic renewal. (The five-year renewal limit also applies to private companies, except that a private company can elect to vary the renewal period, or even give the directors the right to allot new shares for an indefinite period.)

The shareholders of a company with authorized share capital of 4,000,000 shares and issued share capital of 3,500,000 might vote to give their directors powers for one year to allot new shares. The specified limit cannot exceed 500,000 shares, because issuing any more would breach the company's authorized share capital. (To issue more than 500,000 new shares, approval would have to be sought for an increase in the authorized share capital.)

Large public companies, whose issued share capital is usually below their authorized share capital, typically renew the authority of the directors to issue new shares annually, at the annual general meeting. However, the specified limit to the number of new shares that can be issued is restricted, to avoid the risk that new share issues will significantly reduce the proportionate stake of existing shareholders in their company.

Granting the directors some powers to issue new shares can be useful, because it can give the directors freedom to issue new shares to pay for a small acquisition, or to issue new shares under a share option scheme. However, it is usual to restrict the number of new shares the directors can allot to no more than 5% of the current issued share capital of the company.

Note

The Companies Act refers to the 'allotment' of shares, whereas capital market terminology is the 'issue' of new shares. A share is **allotted** when the person to whom it is allotted obtains an unconditional right to be entered in the company's register of members as the owner of the share. The **issue** of shares does not have a legal definition, but is generally taken to occur after allotment, for example when the company issues a letter of allotment or a share certificate to the shareholder.

Pre-emption rights

A pre-emption right is the right to buy something before it is offered for sale to someone else. When a company issues new equity shares (ordinary shares) for cash, existing shareholders are given pre-emption rights by section 89(1) of the Companies Act 1985, in proportion to their existing shareholding.

For example, suppose the directors of a quoted company with 4,000,000 shares in issue want to raise about £7,000,000 to invest in new capital projects. The current share price might be £8, which means that in theory, the company (with shareholder approval) could issue 875,000 new shares at £8 each and allot them to new investors. However, the existing shareholders have pre-emption rights, and any new shares must first be offered to the existing shareholders in proportion to their current shareholding. The issue price in a 'rights issue' of new shares is usually set below the current market price, and in this example, if the issue price is fixed at £7, the company would issue 1,000,000 new shares to raise £7,000,000. The existing shareholders would therefore be offered one new share for every four shares they held. This would be a '1 for 4 rights issue'. It is called a rights issue because it gives pre-emption rights to the existing shareholders.

In a rights issue, the company cannot offer any new shares to other investors until the acceptance period for the offer (which must be at least 21 days) has expired. During this time, shareholders must decide whether to take up their rights to buy the new shares, or to renounce their rights to the allotment of the shares in favour of another person. When a quoted company makes a rights issue, the rights can be sold in the stock market. Since the issue price for the new shares should be lower than the current share price, rights should have real value. Anyone purchasing rights in the stock market acquires the right to subscribe for the new shares. (Shareholders could also ignore a rights issue, and neither take up their rights nor sell them. In these circumstances the company might sell the rights on their behalf at the end of the acceptance period, but is not obliged to do so.)

Pre-emption rights do not apply when new shares are issued for anything other than cash.

Disapplication of pre-emption rights

Shareholders can vote (by special resolution) to disapply their pre-emption rights, and give the directors power to offer new shares to other investors to raise cash.

Typically, when the directors of a public company seek permission from their shareholders to allot new shares up to a specified limit, they must also seek shareholder approval for a disapplication of their pre-emption rights at the same time.

In practice, the ordinary resolution granting the directors powers to allot shares and the special resolution for the disapplication of the pre-emption rights of shareholders will be combined in a single special resolution. This might be worded along the following lines:

'Special resolution: That the directors be and are hereby given power to allot equity securities for cash pursuant to their general authority for the purposes of Section 80 of the Companies Act 1985 as if subsection 1 of Section 89 of the said Act did not apply to such allotment, provided this power shall be limited to the allotment of equity securities up to an aggregate nominal amount of £475,680, representing 5% of the issued share capital, and shall expire (unless previously revoked, varied or extended) on the earlier of the conclusion of the Annual General Meeting of the Company to be held in 200X and 30 June 200X.'

What this means is that shareholders would allow the directors to allot (issue) new shares up to an amount equal to 5% of the issued share capital, without needing to be concerned about their pre-emption rights.

8.10   The UK Listing Rules

In addition to complying with company legislation, companies whose shares are listed (and traded on the main market of the London Stock Exchange) must also comply with the UK Listing Rules. The Rules support the company legislation, but are broader and more extensive.

When a company wants its shares to be traded on the London Stock Exchange, it must apply for the shares to be accepted on to the Official List ('listed'). Its application is made to the UK Listing Authority (UKLA), which is a department of the Financial Services Authority (FSA). The FSA is given responsibility for the Official List under the Financial Services and Markets Act 2000. In addition, the company applying for admission of its securities to the Official List must also apply to the London Stock Exchange (LSE) for the securities to be admitted to trading on the exchange. A condition of being accepted on to the Official List is that the securities must also be admitted to trading on the LSE. The Listing Rules apply to all types of securities, including share warrants and bonds as well as shares.

The rules for applying for admission to the Official List are contained in The Listing Rules, which are issued by the UKLA. The Listing Rules apply to all listed companies (all companies with securities on the Official List) and to companies that are seeking to 'float' their shares on the London Stock Exchange and so obtain a listing for the first time. A large part of the Rules deals with the application for admission of securities to the Official List, covering matters such as:

● Conditions that must be fulfilled before an application will be acceptable.

● Information that must be provided by the company or its advisers, and made available to the public.

- Procedures that must be followed in applying for admission to the Official List.

In addition, companies whose securities have been admitted to the Official List must comply with certain continuing obligations.

The UK Listing Rules and corporate governance

This text does not describe the UK Listing Rules in detail, nor the various ways in which a company might offer its securities to the investing public. The focus of interest is on the relevance of the Listing Rules to corporate governance.

An aim of good corporate governance, **from the point of view of public policy**, should be to create and sustain public confidence in the financial markets, by reducing investor risk. If people believe that public companies are well-governed and well-regulated, they will be more likely to invest in the stock market because they will feel less at risk of a 'rip off' by unscrupulous companies.

Within the broader regulatory and supervisory system, there are some Listing Rules relating to corporate governance. These are mainly contained in the rules relating to the basic conditions for listing, the continuing obligations for listed companies, and rules relating to transactions with related parties. These are described below.

In addition, a **Combined Code on Corporate Governance** is included as an appendix to the Listing Rules. The Code, which is described in detail in Chapter 10, sets out certain principles of good corporate governance, and a code of best practice. It does not form part of the Listing Rules, and compliance by listed companies with the Code is not compulsory. However, it has the support of the UK Listing Authority, the London Stock Exchange and the associations of investment institutions, and strong pressure is brought to bear on listed companies to comply.

Without making the Combined Code compulsory, the Listing Rules give it strong backing by forcing listed companies to disclose and explain their non-compliance. Every UK listed company is required by the Listing Rules to include in its annual report and accounts:

- a narrative statement of how it has applied the Code's principles of good corporate governance, containing sufficient explanations to allow shareholders to evaluate how these principles have been applied, and

- a statement as to whether or not it has complied throughout the accounting period with the code of best practice.

A company that has not complied with all of the Code, or has applied the Code for only part of the accounting period, must specify which Code provisions it has not complied with, where relevant for what part of the period the non-compliance lasted, and give reasons for the non-compliance.

The Listing Rules also contain requirements relating to the disclosure of directors' remuneration. These are described in Chapter 10.

The UK Listing Rules: conditions for listing

Companies applying to have their securities admitted to the Official List must comply with certain conditions for listing. The purpose of these conditions is to protect the interests of potential investors in the securities, so are of relevance for corporate governance. The conditions for listing are not set out in full here, but conditions relating to the directors, the marketability of the shares, and to any controlling shareholder are worth noting.

The directors and senior management of the company applying for a listing must collectively have enough expertise and experience to manage the company's business. Because the directors will be running the company, it is clearly essential to have a suitably qualified management team in which investors can have some trust with the investment of their money. The UK Listing Authority will look at the experience and the expertise of the directors who have been appointed at the time the company makes its application for listing. However, there is no formal system for monitoring this ongoing experience and expertise of the board after listing, when the board personnel could well change, other than the requirements for new directors to obtain approval for their appointment from the shareholders at the next annual general meeting, and for existing directors to stand for re-election at least once every three years.

Another condition for listing is that the applicant company must ensure that each director is free of any conflict of interest between his duties to the company and his private interests, unless the company can demonstrate that there is no risk of damage to the company's interests. If a conflict of interest exists, the UK Listing Authority must be consulted as soon as possible. A conflict of interest would arise, for example, if the director of a construction company were to be appointed to the board of another similar independent construction company (with which his other company might compete for business contracts).

Yet another condition for listing is that there should be a reasonable prospect for an active secondary market in the securities after the listing. To be listed, securities must also be admitted to trading on the London Stock Exchange, which gives them a secondary market to trade in. The shares must also be freely transferable, without restrictions on the right to buy and sell them. In addition, a minimum proportion of the shares must be 'in public hands', to create a potential market of sufficient size. A sufficient proportion is usually considered to be at least 25%, although a lower percentage will be acceptable if the market can operate properly with a lower amount.

A company applying for a listing might have a controlling shareholder. A controlling shareholder is defined for this purpose as someone holding 30% or more of the voting rights, or who is able to control the appointment of a majority of the directors. Where there is a controlling shareholder, a condition for listing is that all transactions and relationships between the company and its controlling shareholder must be at arm's length and on a normal commercial basis. The purpose of this rule, which is also a continuing obligation on companies after admission to listing, is to protect the interests of the other shareholders.

The Listing Rules: continuing obligations

A listed company must comply with certain continuing obligations once its securities have been admitted to listing. These include requirements as to the provision of information to the public and to shareholders, and rights between shareholders.

A company must announce without delay to the market any major new development that is not public knowledge and which could affect the market price of its shares, and also certain board decisions on dividends and profits. (There is a procedure for reporting news to the market through an official reporting service and on to information providers such as Reuters and Bloomberg.) A company must also notify changes in shareholdings of its 'major' shareholders, who are shareholders with at least either 3% or 10% of the shares, depending on circumstances.

The continuing obligations reinforce the legal requirement of companies to inform shareholders of the meetings they are entitled to attend and to enable them to exercise their right to vote. A form for proxy voting must be sent out with the notice convening the general meeting.

There are requirements in the continuing obligations about the rights between shareholders. A company with listed shares 'must ensure equality of treatment for all holders of such shares who are in the same position'. The continuing obligations also repeat the Companies Act rules on the pre-emption rights of shareholders and the disapplication of pre-emption rights subject to shareholder approval.

The Listing Rules: transactions with related parties

The Listing Rules provide some safeguards against current or recent directors of a listed company, or a substantial shareholders, taking advantage of their position. The Rules require that any proposed 'transaction with a related party' must first be notified to and approved by the shareholders in general meeting, where the related party must not be allowed to vote.

A related party is a current director, a person who has been a director within the previous 12 months, a substantial shareholder (controlling 10% or more of the votes) or an associate of any of these persons. The rule applies to directors and recent directors of a subsidiary or a parent company, as well as directors and recent directors of the company itself. An 'associate' includes the individual's family or a company in which the individual or his or her family have an interest of 30% or more.

A proposed related-party transaction must be described in a circular sent to the shareholders, giving sufficient information to allow shareholders to evaluate the effects of the transaction on the company. Shareholder approval must be obtained at a general meeting before the transaction may proceed.

The purpose of these rules is to prevent individuals or major shareholders exploiting their position to benefit at the expense of the company and the (other) shareholders. For example, a director of a listed company might own the freehold of a property the company uses, and enter discussions with his fellow directors about selling the property to the company. The main risk to the company is that the property might be sold for an inflated price, and the Listing Rules include special provisions for the sale of property or private company shares about obtaining a proper independent valuation and informing shareholders of this value.

8.11 The capital of the company and its maintenance

Dividends

Rules on dividends are included in the articles of association. Table A articles include the following specifications.

- A company may declare a dividend in a general meeting, by means of an ordinary resolution.

- The shareholders cannot vote to declare a dividend higher than the amount proposed by the directors. They can vote to approve the dividend proposed by the directors, or to reduce it.

- The directors may declare an interim dividend without shareholder approval if they consider this to be justified.

In practice, the directors will usually declare an interim dividend for the first half of the financial year, and propose a final dividend for the year, for approval by the shareholders at the annual general meeting.

However, there are restrictions on the amount of dividends a company can pay out.

Capital maintenance

The capital of a company is provided by its shareholders. In accounting terms, shareholder capital is shown in a company's balance sheet as:

- share capital at nominal value (face value), and

- a number of reserves, such as the share premium account, capital redemption reserve, revaluation reserve and profit and loss account reserve.

Some capital is non-distributable because it must be kept within the company to maintain the size of its capital. This acts as a form of protection to lenders to the company and other creditors. Another way of looking at shareholder capital is to divide it into:

- non-distributable capital, which includes the share capital of the company (at nominal value) and non-distributable reserves, and

- distributable profits, which include the profit and loss account reserve.

A simplified example might help to illustrate the requirement for capital maintenance. Suppose that when a company is set up, it issues 1,000 shares of £1 each, at a price of £3 per share. The balance sheet of the company would be:

	£
Cash	<u>3,000</u>
Ordinary shares of £1 each	1,000
Share premium account	<u>2,000</u>
Share capital and reserves	<u>3,000</u>

Now suppose the company takes out a bank loan of £2,500 and uses this to buy an item of equipment. The position of the company would now be as follows.

	£
Equipment	2,500
Cash	<u>3,000</u>
Total assets	5,500
Bank loan	<u>(2,500)</u>
Assets minus liabilities	<u>3,000</u>
Ordinary shares of £1 each	1,000
Share premium account	<u>2,000</u>
Share capital and reserves	<u>3,000</u>

The bank might consider that its loan to the company is safe because the company has capital of £3,000. However, suppose the company is allowed to make dividend payments 'distributions') to its shareholders out of capital and decided to pay a dividend of £2,000. The revised balance sheet would now be as follows.

	£
Equipment	2,500
Cash	<u>1,000</u>
Total assets	3,500
Bank loan	<u>(2,500)</u>
Assets minus liabilities	<u>1,000</u>
Ordinary shares of £1 each	<u>1,000</u>

The bank will now feel that the credit risk is much higher. The bank loan is financing a much greater proportion of what is left of the company.

To prevent this type of situation arising, company law forbids a company from making a distribution (paying dividends) except out of profits. In the example above, the company would be required to maintain capital of at least £3,000, and could only pay a dividend out of any profits it has made.

The non-distributable reserves of a company include:

- the share premium account

- the capital redemption reserve, if there is one

- any other reserve that the company is prohibited from distribution, either by law or by the company's memorandum or articles of association.

Distributable profits

Section 263 of the Companies Act 1985 states that: 'A company shall not make a distribution except out of profits available for the purpose.'

The term 'make a distribution' essentially means 'pay a dividend', but the Act defines a distribution as any form of distribution of a company's assets to its shareholders, whether in cash or otherwise. For example, a distribution could be made to shareholders in the form of physical assets, such as stocks.

Distributable profits are defined as the accumulated realized profits of the company (to the extent that these have not already been paid out as dividends) minus its accumulated realized losses. For example, suppose that a company makes a profit after taxation of £4 million in the current year, but the company has accumulated losses from previous years of £3 million. The maximum distribution the company can make in the current year is therefore £1 million. In effect, the accumulated losses have to be wiped out by accumulated profits before a dividend can be paid.

'Realized' profits and losses are profits and losses that are recognized as having occurred in accordance with generally accepted accounting practice. Some profits or losses might be accounted for before they are realized, and so appear in the balance sheet of a company as unrealized profits or losses. For example, suppose that a company owns a freehold property that it bought for £2 million but which is now valued at £3.5 million. The company might decide to revalue the property, and show it in the balance sheet at its current value. If the property is revalued by £1.5 million to £3.5 million, there will be an unrealized gain of £1.5 million. This will be shown in a revaluation reserve in the balance sheet. It is an unrealized gain because the company has not sold the property. Until the property is sold, there is no realized profit, and the company cannot distribute the profit as a dividend to its shareholders.

In the case of a *public company*, the Companies Act makes a further restriction on the distribution of its assets by a public company. A company may make a distribution to its shareholders only if its net assets (total assets minus total liabilities) is not less than the total of its called up share capital and non-distributable reserves, and the distribution would not reduce net assets below this total.

Capitalization issues and capital maintenance

A company might occasionally make a capitalization issue of new shares. A capitalization issue, which might be called a bonus issue or a scrip issue, involves the distribution of free new shares to existing shareholders in proportion to the number of shares they currently hold. For example, a company might make a 1 for 4 bonus issue, and distribute one free new share to its shareholders for every four shares they currently hold. When a capitalization issue occurs, a company is allowed to make the distribution out of non-distributable reserves (the share premium account). This is permitted by law because the total non-distributable capital of the company is maintained.

For example suppose that a company has 1,000,000 shares of £1 in issue and a share premium account of £800,000. It might decide to make a 1 for 2 bonus issue, and issue 500,000 free new shares to its shareholders. It can make this distribution out of the non-distributable share premium account, and after the issue has been made, total share capital will be 1,500,000 shares of £1 and a share premium account of £300,000. The principle of capital maintenance has not been violated, because non-distributable capital remains £1,800,000 in total.

However, a capitalization issue can also be made, wholly or in part, out of distributable profits. When this happens, however, the distributable profits that have been used to issue new shares cease to be distributable, because they now form part of the share capital. For example, suppose that a company with issued share capital of 1,000,000 ordinary shares of £1 each also has a share premium account of £200,000 and distributable profit and loss reserves of £700,000. If the company decides to make a 1 for 2 bonus issue, it might decide to use up the share premium account for the purpose, and £300,000 of the distributable profits. After the bonus issue, the company will have issued share capital of £1,500,000 and just £400,000 of profit and loss reserves.

Share repurchases and capital maintenance

At any time, a company may cancel shares that have been authorized but not yet issued. For example, if a company has authorized share capital of 3,000,000 shares and issued share capital of 2,000,000, it can reduce its authorized share capital (with the approval of the shareholders) by up to 1,000,000 shares. This would not constitute a reduction in share capital.

As a general rule, a company cannot reduce its share capital by cancelling shares that have already been issued. The issued share capital is part of the long-term capital provided by the shareholders, and creditors of the company will expect this capital to remain in place. A shareholder wanting to cash in his investment normally has to do so by selling the shares to someone else.

However, under certain conditions, a company is permitted to reduce its share capital by cancelling issued shares. The conditions are such that, although the issued share capital is reduced, the total of non-distributable capital (issued share capital plus non-distributable reserves) remains unchanged. The principle of capital maintenance is upheld, even when shares are repurchased and cancelled. This is achieved by means of a transfer of funds to a 'capital redemption reserve' account, which is a non-distributable reserve.

A company might decide that it has too many shares in issue, and start a programme of repurchasing and cancelling some shares. The repurchase of its shares by a company must be permitted by the articles of association, and approved by the shareholders in a general meeting.

A public limited company might decide, for example, to repurchase up to 1,000,000 of its own £1 ordinary shares by means of stock market purchases. Suppose that it buys 1,000,000 shares for a total price of £2,500,000 and cancels them. It would probably use its distributable reserves to make the repurchase, and would be required to transfer to a capital redemption reserve account an amount equal to the nominal value of the shares repurchased and cancelled. In this example, the company's holding of cash would be reduced by £2,500,000 (to make the purchases) and distributable reserves would also be reduced by £2,500,000. In addition, share capital would be reduced by £1,000,000 and the capital redemption reserve would be increased by £1,000,000. Non-distributable capital remains unchanged.

Assets	£
Cash (used to buy back shares)	- 2,500,000
Share capital and reserves	
Share capital	- 1,000,000
Capital redemption reserve (non-distributable)	+ 1,000,000
Distributable profits	- 2,500,000
Total change in share capital and reserves	- 2,500,000

The share capital is lower by £1,000,000 but the non-distributable capital redemption reserve has been increased by £1,000,000, leaving the total of non-distributable capital unchanged.

8.12   Conclusion

A broad framework for corporate governance is provided by company law and the constitution (memorandum and articles of association) of a company.

● The law gives a company a separate legal personality, which detaches it from its owners, the shareholders. The law also makes a distinction between the owners of a company and its managers.

● The division of power between the owners and the managers is also established by law and the company's memorandum and articles. Shareholders have relatively little power over decision-making, and therefore rely on the directors to run the company and make decisions that are in the best interests of the shareholders.

- Shareholders have some rights that limit the risk of directors ignoring their interests, but it is questionable whether these rights are sufficiently strong, or whether they can be exercised easily.

- The law also gives some protection to the creditors of a company, by applying the concept of capital maintenance and prohibiting a company from making distributions except out of distributable profits.

9

DIRECTORS

After reading this chapter, you should:

- Understand the legal duty that directors owe to their company

- Understand the consequences of a breach of duty by a director, and the circumstances in which a director might be removed from office or disqualified

- Understand, in broad outline, what the statutory duties of a director are.

9.1 The powers of directors as an issue in corporate governance

The powers of the directors are set out in the articles of association. These apply to both executive and non-executive directors. Table A article 70 states that subject to the provisions of the Companies Act 1985, the memorandum and articles and any directions given to them by a special resolution of the members, the directors 'may exercise all the powers of the company'. Article 72 goes on to state that:

- 'the directors may delegate any of their powers to any committee consisting of one or more directors', and

- 'they may also delegate to any managing director or any director holding any other executive office such of their powers as they consider desirable to be exercised by him.'

The standard articles of association therefore provide for the directors collectively to be the main power holders in a company, although the board can delegate its powers to a managing director and individual executive directors.

This raises the question of what is to stop the board of directors running the company in their own interests? Or, what is to prevent a powerful managing director running the company for his or her personal benefit? In comparison with the directors, other stakeholders in a company, even the shareholders who own it, would seem to have relatively little say in how the company is run. This is a problem that goes to the heart of many concerns about practice in corporate governance.

To some extent, the actions that directors might take are constrained by their duties to the company. This chapter looks at what those duties are, and the possible consequences that could arise when a director is in breach of duty. A question to consider, however, is whether the legal duties of directors are a sufficient restraint on the improper exercise of their power.

It is important to bear in mind, however, that the directors of a company might also be managers, operating in an executive role. The duties of directors, as established in law, apply to both executive and non-executive directors. Do not confuse the responsibilities of management with the legal duties of directors. Managers do not have statutory duties, nor powers under the articles of association: their relationship with the company is determined by their contract of employment and other aspects of the law (particularly employment law).

9.2   Duty of directors to the company

The duties of directors in law are **to the company itself**, not its shareholders, employees or any person external to the company.

Before looking in detail at the duties of directors, it might be useful to think about the concept of duty more broadly, by comparing duties owed by other individuals or groups.

A company is a legal person, but is not human. There are not many examples of individuals owing a duty to something inanimate. Individuals might be expected to show **loyalty** to something, such as their country, a concept or even a football club, but there is no **duty** of loyalty. Military personnel have a duty to their country, and it could be argued that some professionals such as solicitors have a duty to their profession to act ethically. Duty is more commonly owed to individuals or a group of people. Doctors have a duty to act ethically in their work, but most would probably argue that their prime duty is to their patients.

The duty of directors to their company could lead on to a supposition that the directors must therefore owe a duty to the owners of the company (the shareholders) and possibly also to the employees or another stakeholder group. Oddly perhaps, this is not the case. The 'duty' of directors to shareholders and employees will be considered in more detail later.

When a person is guilty of a breach of duty, there is often a mechanism for calling him or her to account, in a court or in front of a judicial panel. In other words, there is an established disciplinary procedure, with a recognized set of punishments for misbehaviour. With directors, disciplinary mechanisms exist but it might be argued that they are not easy to apply in practice, except in fairly extreme circumstances. The effectiveness of controls over the misbehaviour of directors is therefore a corporate governance issue.

Fiduciary duties of directors

'Fiduciary' is a word meaning given in trust. Directors hold a position of trust in their company, because they make contracts on its behalf and control the company's property. Since they hold a position of trust and are quasi-trustees of their company, they have fiduciary duties. These duties are to the company, not its shareholders.

If a director acts in breach of his fiduciary duties, legal action against him can be taken by the company. In practice, 'the company' would need to be a majority of the board of directors, a majority of the shareholders or a controlling shareholder. (An individual director or shareholder can apply to the court to have the transaction by the director declared void, but the court will generally decide to refer the matter for decision to a general meeting of the company.)

Where the court finds that director is in breach of his or her fiduciary duties, it might order him to compensate the company for any loss suffered and account to the company for any personal profit that he has made from his actions.

The tests of whether a director is in breach of his fiduciary duties are as follows:

- The transaction carried out by the director should be reasonably incidental to the business of the company.

- The transaction should have been carried out with honesty and sincerity ('bona fide').

- The transaction should have been made for the benefit of the company.

A transaction that would put a director in breach of his fiduciary duties is one giving rise to a conflict between the interests of the company and the personal interests of the director. A director has a fiduciary duty to avoid a conflict of interest, and must not obtain any personal benefit or profit from any such transaction without the consent of the company. In other words, a director must not make a **secret profit** from any transaction with the company in which he has a personal interest.

If a director obtains a personal profit from a transaction, by virtue of his position as a director, he must account to the company for the profit he makes, unless he discloses all the facts to the shareholders in a general meeting and obtains their approval for his action. Shareholder approval is required, rather than approval of the board of directors. If shareholder approval is obtained, he can retain the profit. Any contract made by the director in breach of his fiduciary duty and not approved by the shareholders is voidable. ('Voidable' means that it is not automatically void but can be made void if desired).

An example of breach of fiduciary duty is illustrated by the case *Industrial Development Consultants Ltd v Cooley* [1972]. Cooley, a highly-regarded architect, was the managing director of a firm of consultants that advised on construction projects in the gas industry. A potential client had plans for new construction work, but said that it would not use the services of the firm. Cooley recognized, however, that the client might award the work to him personally. He notified the board of his company that he was ill, and persuaded them to release him from his contract of employment. He then obtained the work from the client. The company took him to court, claiming that he was in breach of his fiduciary duty and must account for his profits. The court agreed, even though the client would not have awarded the work to the firm.

In the commercial world, it is inevitable that many directors will have a potential conflict of interest, direct or indirect, with their company. Directors are permitted to enter into contracts with their company, under certain conditions, but must not make a secret profit. The Table

A articles of association allow a director, provided he has disclosed the nature of his material interest, be a party to any transaction with the company.

Example

A company wishes to take a lease on a property owned by one of its directors. The director would be aware of the company's interest in the property from his position as director, so a fiduciary duty arises. The lease agreement would need the prior approval of a majority of the shareholders in a general meeting.

The company might then enter a ten-year lease agreement, but decide three years later that it wants to buy the freehold on the property. The purchase would be a different transaction, and the director would need to obtain shareholder approval again.

Duty of skill and care

A distinction is made between the fiduciary duties of directors and a duty of skill and care to their company that they have at common law. A director should not act negligently in carrying out his duties, and a director could be personally liable for any losses suffered due to his or her negligence. The basic standard required is the skill and care that would be exercised by a reasonable man in looking after his own affairs. This standard is not particularly high.

- A director will, however, be expected to show a degree of technical skill that would reasonably be expected from someone of his experience and expertise. The standard will therefore vary according to circumstances. For example, if the finance director of a computer software company is a qualified accountant, he would not be expected to have the skills of a software engineer, but he would be expected to have a reasonable degree of technical skill as an accountant.

- A director should attend board meetings when he is able to, but is not required at other times to concern himself with the affairs of the company. The duties of a director are intermittent in nature. If the director holds an executive position in the company, with a service contract, the situation is different because he carries out his management duties as an **employee** of the company, not as a director.

- Unless there are particular grounds for suspicion, a director is entitled to leave the routine conduct of the company's affairs to the management. If the management seems honest, the directors may trust them and rely on the information they provide. It is not a requirement of the duty of skill and care to monitor management more closely.

The courts are generally reluctant to condemn business decisions taken by directors that appear, with the benefit of hindsight, to be bad ones. It is possible to exercise reasonable skill and care, but still make a bad mistake or error of judgement.

Wrongful trading and the standard of duty and care

In the UK, the expected standard of duty and care has been partly defined in legal cases relating to wrongful trading. Directors may be liable under section 214 of the Insolvency Act 1986 for wrongful trading by the company, when they know (or ought to have known) that their company would be unable to avoid insolvency and liquidation, but nevertheless allowed the company to continue trading. In such cases, the liquidator of the company can apply to the court for the director to be held personally liable for negligence, and required to make a contribution to the assets of the company in the liquidation. In some legal cases, the judge has likened a director's duty under section 214 to the duty of skill and care at common law.

9.3 Breach of duty by directors

A director may be personally liable for a breach of fiduciary duty or the duty of skill and care. Any legal action against one or more directors would normally be taken by the company (a majority of the board or a majority of the shareholders). If held liable for a breach of duty, a director may be required to make good the loss suffered by the company, and, as mentioned earlier, would be required to account to the company for any secret profit he has made. Where a director has taken property of the company, the company will be able to recover it.

The company would also have the right to avoid a contract involving a conflict of interest for a director, but it could not both avoid the contract and claim any losses suffered from the director concerned.

For a legal action by the company against a director to succeed, on the grounds of a lack of skill and care, the company will have to prove that *serious* negligence has occurred. It would not be sufficient to show that if a director had been a bit more careful, a loss could have been avoided.

Since it is the company that would seek remedies against a director for a breach of duty, the company can also ratify an action by a director who is in breach of duty. Ratification, which is giving retrospective approval, would require a majority vote of the shareholders (an ordinary resolution in a general meeting of the company). The company would have to give shareholders full disclosure of the facts, to allow them to reach their decision. If the director or directors concerned are also shareholders, they would be entitled to use their votes in the general meeting in their own support.

The Companies Act 1985 also gives the court the power to grant relief to a director from his liability for breach of duty if, in the court's opinion, the director acted reasonably and honestly.

9.4 Restrictions on directors taking financial advantage

Directors might use their position in the company to extract personal financial advantages. There are some legal restraints. Shareholder approval is required for any transaction between the company and a director involving the transfer of property above a certain value. If shareholder approval is not obtained, the transaction is voidable, and the director will be liable either to account to the company for any personal profit from the transaction, or to indemnify the company for any loss it has suffered.

There are also restrictions on loans to a director by the company, to prevent a situation in which the directors simply take money out of the company with an undertaking to pay it back at some time in the future. Directors of stock market companies could also be liable under the Financial Services and Markets Act 2000 for 'market abuse', which could involve using their position and inside knowledge to profit from trading in the shares of the company. However, there are no legal restraints on the size of the salary or total remuneration package that a director might be awarded. The Companies Act 1985 simply requires that the annual report and accounts should include certain information about directors' remuneration, and that the service contracts of directors should be available for inspection by shareholders.

Directors' remuneration is a contentious issue in corporate governance, and is considered in more detail in the next chapter.

9.5   The removal of a director from office

The shareholders of a company will have rights under the articles of association to remove a director from office, and they could choose not to re-elect a director retiring by rotation. In addition, if the shareholders are dissatisfied with a director, they have the right under the Companies Act 1985 to remove a director from office by an ordinary resolution in a general meeting.

The shareholders proposing to remove a director from office have the right to call a general meeting of the company, provided they represent at least 5% of the total voting rights. The board of directors might be hostile to an attempt to remove one or more of their number from office, but they are prevented by the legislation from refusing to call or hold a general meeting. In practice, however, it would require extreme circumstances for a group of shareholders to seek to remove a director from office without the support of the rest of the board.

Disqualification of directors

A director might be disqualified. On disqualification he or she would vacate office immediately. The main grounds for disqualification would be either under the provisions of the articles of association or disqualification by the court under the Company Directors' Disqualification Act 1986. In addition, an undischarged bankrupt cannot act as director, except with permission of the court.

Disqualification under the articles

The articles of association might provide for the disqualification of a director under a variety of circumstances. The Table A articles include provisions that a director should vacate office if he or she becomes bankrupt or is mentally ill. It also provides for a director to be removed from office by the rest of the board if he or she has been absent without permission from board meetings for over six months and the board decides that removal from office would be appropriate.

Disqualification by the court

A director might be disqualified by the court. Depending on the reasons for disqualification, the director might or might not have personal liability for the company's debts.

Disqualification without personal liability for the company's debts could arise in any of the following situations.

- The individual has been convicted of an indictable offence in connection with the promotion, formation, management or liquidation of a company, or with a receivership. There have been cases where a director has been disqualified for being tried and convicted of an indictable offence under the health and safety at work legislation.

- It appears that the individual has been persistently in default and breach of company law, by failing to submit any return, accounts or document to the Registrar of Companies. Three or more defaults within a five-year period are sufficient to count as a 'persistent' breach of company law.

- It appears during the course of winding up a company that the individual has been guilty of fraudulent trading or some other type of fraud, while acting as a director. An **appearance** of fraud is sufficient for the court to disqualify the individual. In addition, if an individual is found guilty of fraudulent trading, he or she could also be personally liable for the company's debts. This is explained later.

- When a company becomes insolvent, and the conduct of a director makes him unfit to be involved in the management of the company, the Secretary of State for the Department of Trade and Industry (DTI) might apply to the court for the person to be disqualified. An allegation of unfitness originates with an administrator or liquidator of the company, who contacts the DTI. The DTI will then investigate the complaint and decide whether an application to the court should be made for a disqualification order.

- In certain circumstances, the DTI might carry out an investigation into a company that is not insolvent. If, in the course of such an investigation, it comes to the view that a director is unfit to manage the company, the DTI may apply to the court for a disqualification order.

Examples of offences for which directors have been disqualified from office by the court include insider dealing in the shares of the company, a failure to keep proper accounting records, and making a loan to an associated company on uncommercial terms.

Disqualification by the court with personal liability

The law makes a distinction between the crime of fraudulent trading (criminal law) and the personal liability of individual directors for fraudulent or wrongful trading (civil law). The

Insolvency Act 1986 allows a court to disqualify a director who has been involved in either fraudulent trading or wrongful trading when the company is insolvent. In these circumstances, the disqualified individual could be held personally liable for the debts of the company. However, only the liquidator of the company can apply to the court for a declaration of civil liability.

Fraudulent trading occurs when, during the course of winding up a company, business is carried on with the intent of defrauding creditors 'or for any fraudulent purpose' (section 213 of the Insolvency Act 1986). Examples of fraudulent trading are falsification of the company's books of account, making a material omission of fact in a statement about the company's affairs, and making a false representation to creditors with a view to persuading them to come to an agreement with the company.

For the court to disqualify the director and hold him or her personally liable for the company's debts under section 213, it is necessary to prove fraud. This could be difficult. In contrast, a lower burden of proof is required for wrongful trading, under section 214 of the Act. The court will disqualify a director from office and hold him or her liable for wrongful trading if **negligence** is proved, rather than criminal conduct. Wrongful trading occurs when the director of a company knew, or should have known, before official winding up procedures began, that the company would go into insolvent liquidation but did not take enough steps to minimize the potential loss to creditors.

Where the court makes the individual liable for debts of the company for fraudulent or wrongful trading, the liability is to the liquidator of the company.

9.6   Statutory duties of directors

Directors themselves (as distinct from their company) do not have many statutory duties and obligations. They are under a duty to take minutes of their meetings and to deliver a copy of the company's report and accounts to the Registrar of Companies. They are also responsible for ensuring that the company makes proper returns to the Registrar, and could be disqualified by the court for a persistent breach of this requirement (see above).

Disclosure obligations

Directors are under an obligation to inform the company of any interests they have in its shares or debentures, and of any change in those interests. This information is held by the company in a register of directors' interests.

There is also a requirement for directors with a direct or indirect personal interest in a contact with the company to declare the interest at a meeting of the board of directors.

Fiduciary duties and directors' responsibilities to employees

Section 309 of the Companies Act 1985 contains a requirement that in performing their functions, one of the matters to which the directors should 'have regard' is the interests of the company's employees in general, as well as the interests of the shareholders. The directors have this duty to the company, not the employees, and it is enforceable in the same way as any other fiduciary duty.

Although the directors should have some regard to the interests of employees, employees themselves do not have the right to enforce this requirement, because the duty of the directors is to the company. In practice, therefore, this 'duty' concerning employees would appear to have limited practical value. It means, for example, that the directors would be carrying out their duties if they made a decision to preserve jobs, if this would also be in the interests of the company. However, they would not be justified in taking a decision to save jobs if by doing so they put the company's financial position at risk.

9.7   Directors and company outsiders

Although the duty of directors is to their company, outsiders could be affected by any breach of duty that occurs. When the directors enter into a contract with an outsider in accordance with the company's articles, the contract is binding on the company. However, when the directors exceed their powers when entering into a contract (for example, because the prior approval of shareholders was required but not obtained), the transaction would, *prima facie*, be void. The term 'irregular contract' is used to describe contracts entered into without proper authority.

A problem with an irregular contract is that if it is void, an outsider entering into the contract in good faith will be unable to enforce it against the company. However, if an irregular contract is enforceable at law, a company has no protection against the risk that its directors could bind the company by entering into a contract contrary to the articles of association.

The legal position is that irregular contracts are binding on a company in some circumstances, but not in others. The Companies Act 1985 provides that where an outsider, acting in good faith, enters into an irregular contract with a company and the contract has been decided on or approved by the board of directors, the contract will be binding on the company. The directors will be liable to the company for any loss suffered. As a consequence of the legislation, irregular contracts are a corporate governance problem, but do not affect third parties.

If a shareholder suspects that the directors are about to enter into a contract without proper authority, because the decision requires the prior approval of the shareholders, he or she can apply to the court for an injunction to restrain them.

9.8   Conclusion

This chapter has focused on the legal duties of directors, and the extent to which these act as a restraint on the ability of directors to run their company without regard to the interests of the shareholders, employees or outsiders. Experience has shown that in many cases, these restraints are inadequate. As it stands, the law on its own does not provide sufficient protection to shareholders, who own the company. It can also be argued that the law provides insufficient protection to other stakeholders, notably employees.

The inadequacy of the law, inevitably, has resulted in pressure for changes and improvements. At the moment, the focus of attention is on a voluntary code of best practice in corporate governance, although the possibility of further legislation in the future cannot be ruled out.

The next chapter describes the corporate governance initiatives in recent years, primarily from a UK perspective but with some reference to the international picture.

10

CORPORATE GOVERNANCE IN THE UK

After reading this chapter, you should:

- Understand the main issues in corporate governance
- Know the history of the development of a code of corporate governance in the UK
- Understand the role in corporate governance of the board collectively and the directors individually
- Understand the significance of risk management and responsible management generally for good corporate governance
- Understand how a risk-based approach to management is encouraged by the corporate governance code in the UK.

Introduction

Because UK law does not provide a sufficiently robust framework for corporate governance, the possibility must exist that in some companies the directors will abuse their powers and get away with it, usually at the expense of their shareholders. When such a possibility exists, it is perhaps not surprising when incidents occur that result in criticism about how a particular company has been governed.

The history to date of corporate governance in the UK has been marked by a series of incidents or situations giving rise to investor concerns, leading to the gradual development by the major financial institutions over time of a code of best practice. The accepted view to date is that a voluntary code, if sensibly applied, will be much more effective than new laws or regulations, and be more flexible.

The focus of attention in corporate governance issues has shifted from time to time, with the problem causing most concern for a while eventually giving way to another. The code of best practice in corporate governance has therefore evolved as each successive concern has resulted in a further addition or amendment to the code. Broadly speaking, however, the main concerns in the UK have been the following.

- Powerful individual executives, perhaps holding the position of both board chairman and chief executive, dominating their company and running it more for their personal benefit than in the interests of the shareholders.

- Misleading and uninformative financial accounts from public companies, so that shareholders cannot properly understand what has been going on in their company, nor the strength (or, more to the point, the weakness) of its financial position. Concerns about the financial accounts leads to concerns about the nature of the relationship between a company and its external auditors. Are the external auditors properly independent, or has a 'cosy relationship' built up with the company, such that the auditors cannot perform their audit function objectively?

- Excessive remuneration for executive directors, when the rewards they are paid are not linked to company performance in the interests of the shareholders.

- Independent non-executive directors, who are appointed to provide a counterbalance to powerful executive directors and to provide the benefit of their experience and know-how to decision-making by the board, but who are often ineffective.

- A concern that companies and their directors are not properly aware of the risks faced by the company, and do not have a robust system of risk management in place. Poor risk management in a company will probably affect the shareholders eventually.

10.1   Corporate governance in the UK

The UK has a code of best practice in corporate governance that applies to all listed UK companies. (These are companies whose shares have been admitted to the Official List and are traded on the main market of the London Stock Exchange.) The code is known as the Combined Code: Principles of Good Governance and Code of Best Practice, or the Combined Code for short. It is included as an appendix to the Listing Rules, which are rules that all listed companies must comply with. However, the Code does not form part of the Listing Rules, but instead has 'semi-official status', in the sense that there is no compulsion on companies to adopt the Code, but there is strong pressure to do so from the City of London institutions. The Combined Code is therefore a framework for voluntary self-regulation by listed companies.

It is helpful to look briefly at the history of developments leading up to the publication of the Combined Code in 1998, beginning with the Cadbury Code in 1992.

10.2   The Cadbury Code

At the instigation of the London Stock Exchange, and following a number of corporate failures in the 1980s, a committee was established, under the chairmanship of Sir Adrian Cadbury, of representatives of financial markets institutions. The task of the committee was to look into financial aspects of corporate governance, amid concerns that annual financial report and accounts of listed companies were often misleading and that, all too often, there was 'window dressing' of profits. The role and effectiveness of the external auditors were also under scrutiny, with doubts expressed about the reliability of a 'clean bill of health' for the company's accounts in the auditors' report.

The main concern at the time was the failure of published financial accounts to reveal the true financial position of the company, and a suspicion that the external auditors were not sufficiently effective in the work they did. The attention of the committee broadened, however, to include other aspects of corporate governance, particularly the functions and the effectiveness of the board of directors. The stated aim of the Cadbury committee was to help to raise standards of corporate governance and confidence in financial reporting and auditing, by setting out what it saw as the respective responsibilities of those involved and what it believed was expected of them.

A matter of particular concern was, in some listed companies, a perceived domination of the board by one individual, or a small group of individuals, and the public perception that these companies were being run for the benefit of the directors in charge rather than in the interests of shareholders.

The committee accepted that it was appropriate for the directors to retain what it described as their 'essential powers', and there should be no question of giving more powers to shareholders. On the other hand, it believed that the directors should be suitably accountable to the shareholders.

At the time of the committee's report, non-executive directors on boards of companies were heavily outnumbered by executive directors, and many non-executives were appointees of major shareholders, and so not independent. There were also doubts about the ability of executive directors to act independently, rather than go along with the opinions of their chief executive or chairman. In a large number of listed companies, the same person held the roles of chairman and chief executive, putting him or her in a position of considerable power in relation to the other executive directors.

The committee's report included a number of recommendations on best practice in corporate governance, which became known as the Cadbury Code. The Code was aimed at UK public limited companies. Many of the recommended practices were already in widespread use, although not in all listed companies. The report recommended that the Code should be **voluntary**, but that quoted companies should be required to state in their annual report and accounts whether they were complying with the provisions of the Code. Any non-compliance with the provisions of the Code should be disclosed. It was also suggested that this statement of compliance should be reviewed by the external auditors before publication.

The London Stock Exchange, which at that time was responsible for the UK Listing Rules, accepted the committee's recommendations, and added to the Listing Rules a requirement for a statement of compliance to be included in the annual report and accounts of listed companies. Although the Code was voluntary, pressure was brought to bear on listed companies, for example by investment bank advisers and institutional investors and their professional associations, to comply with it.

The main provisions of the Cadbury Code dealt with the responsibilities and composition of the board of directors as a whole, and individual board members, but there were also provisions relating to financial reporting and the relationship between a company and its external auditors. An intention was that compliance with the Code should help to achieve a board of independent-minded directors, acting in what they considered to be the best interests of the company.

The board of directors

The Cadbury Code stated that control over the company should be exercised by the board of directors **as a whole**, and not by an individual executive director or chairman, or by a small group of executive directors.

- The board should therefore meet regularly and retain full and effective control over the company. An element of its task should be to monitor the performance of the executive management. Some decisions should, as a matter of course, be referred to the board for a decision, and should not be taken by executive managers. For example, decisions about mergers and takeovers should be reserved for the board. There should also be a formal schedule of matters that are specifically reserved for board decisions, to ensure that control of the company remains firmly in its hands. These provisions were to guard against an all-powerful chief executive or chairman taking major decisions himself or herself, without consulting other board colleagues.

- There should be a clear division of responsibilities at the top of the company. In particular, it will usually be desirable to separate the role of chairman (who is responsible for managing the board) and the chief executive (who is responsible for running the operations of the business). The Code did not state that the same individual should never hold the positions of chairman and chief executive. Instead, it recommended that when these posts were filled by the same individual, there should be a strong independent element on the board to act as a counterweight, with a recognized senior member.

- A board should include a sufficient number of **non-executives** for their views to carry sufficient weight. At the time the Code was published, many listed companies did not have any non-executives at all on their board, and the recommended changes were therefore quite radical. The Code also includes several recommendations to try to ensure their independence and their ability to contribute effectively to decision-making by the board. These are described later.

- The Code also recognized that there will be occasions where a director will need professional advice in order to form an opinion. It therefore recommends that there should be an agreed procedure whereby a director, carrying out his or her duties, should be able to obtain professional advice at the company's expense.

Non-executive directors

The view underlying the Cadbury Code was that the non-executive directors should be able to bring judgement and experience to the deliberations of the board that the executive directors on their own would lack. The Code therefore recommended that the non-executives should bring an independent judgement to bear on issues, and the majority of them should be independent. (A minimum number of non-executives was recommended, but the specific Cadbury recommendation no longer applies.)

To ensure that non-executives should not rely for their tenure in office on one or two individuals, the Code recommends that they should be selected through a formal process, possibly beginning with a nominations committee, but which should also be a matter for the board as a whole. Non-executives should also be appointed for a specific fixed term, and reappointment at the end of that term should not be automatic. The thinking here was that a non-executive appointed by the chairman or the chief executive, and for a long term, might not be sufficiently independent.

The Code includes a number of recommendations to restrain executive pay. These were not particularly stringent, and other requirements have since been introduced.

- The service contract of an executive director should not exceed three years without shareholder approval. (This has since been reduced to 12 months.) A significant aspect of the length of a service contract is that if a director is asked to leave a company, perhaps because of poor performance, he or she might be entitled to payment up to the end of the contract notice period. This would mean, for example, that a director on a three-year rolling contract with an annual salary of £150,000 might be entitled to a 'golden handshake' of £450,000 for leaving.

- The pay of executive directors should be subject to recommendations of a remuneration committee of the board, made up wholly or mainly of non-executives.

- The Code included recommendations for some disclosure of the emoluments of directors. These disclosures were not particularly extensive, and the Cadbury recommendations have since been superseded.

Reporting controls and the Cadbury recommendations

The official name of the Cadbury Committee was the Committee on the Financial Aspects of Corporate Governance. Not surprisingly, the Cadbury Code addressed concerns about public confidence in the reliability of published accounts, and included recommendations about financial reporting and the accountability of the board to the shareholders. These recommendations should be seen against a background of the spectacular and unexpected financial collapse of a number of UK listed companies at around the time the committee was doing its work.

- The board has a **duty** to present a balanced and understandable picture of the company's position in reporting to shareholders. The directors should include in their report a **statement that the business is a going concern**. The implication of this recommendation is that, before approving the report, each director should take steps to reassure himself or herself that the company is actually a going concern and not on the brink of insolvency.

- The board should ensure that an objective and professional relationship is maintained with the external auditors. There should be an **audit committee** of the board, including at least three non-executive directors, with written terms of reference. It was envisaged that the relationship between the board and the external auditors would be maintained largely through this committee.

The Cadbury Code also included a radical recommendation that the directors should report to the shareholders on the company's entire system of internal control, not just its financial controls. The board would therefore be accountable to the shareholders for risk management generally, not just the quality of financial reporting. The reaction to this proposal was initially quite hostile, and the Code was watered down to stating that the directors should report on internal financial controls only. The board's responsibility for the company's entire system of risk management was subsequently revived by the Hampel report and written into the Combined Code in 1998.

10.3　The Greenbury Report: Directors' remuneration

After the Cadbury Code was implemented, the focus of attention switched to directors' pay and benefits, which were widely regarded as excessive. The public press regularly condemned 'fat cat' directors who paid themselves enormous salaries even when their companies performed badly. The pay of directors in recently-privatized nationalized industries were subject to particularly heavy public criticism. An even greater concern for institutional investors was that executive directors' pay was not properly linked to company performance in the interests of the shareholders. In other words, when a company did well, the directors and the shareholders would all benefit, which is fair enough. However, when a company did badly, the shareholders suffered but the directors did not: their remuneration was unaffected. This did not seem appropriate.

A study group was established under the chairmanship of Sir Richard Greenbury to look into directors' remuneration. The recommendations of the committee, published in 1995, were known as the Greenbury Code. Unlike the Cadbury Code, which was widely welcomed, the Greenbury Code had a mixed reception. Many people took the view that the Code did not do enough to address the problem that many directors were highly rewarded for performance that did little or nothing to promote the objectives of the company and to benefit shareholders.

The recommendations of Greenbury were as follows.

- A **remuneration committee** of the board should decide the remuneration of the executive directors. The committee should consist entirely of non-executive directors, so that no executive director should have the responsibility for setting his own remuneration, or the remuneration of executive colleagues.

- The maximum notice period in an executive director's service contract should normally be 12 months, compared to the three years maximum recommended by Cadbury. (In practice, many executive directors with existing three-year rolling contracts were subsequently persuaded to agree to a reduction to a 12-month notice period in their service contract.) The report added, however, that notice periods of up to two years might be reasonable in some circumstances. In exceptional circumstances, such as offering an enticement to an individual to join the board, a notice period in excess of two years might even be justified.

- The report included extensive recommendations on the disclosure of information about the company's remuneration policy and the remuneration of individual directors. A report on directors' **remuneration policy** should be included in the annual report and accounts, giving details on remuneration levels and how these compare with other, similar companies, the main component elements of remuneration, pension provision, directors' service contracts and compensation for loss of office.

- All **bonus schemes** should depend on **satisfactory performance criteria**. In other words, incentive or bonus payments to directors should be performance-related. Any long-term incentive schemes should be submitted to the shareholders, in advance, for approval. A problem with this recommendation was that it did not provide rules or practical guidelines for deciding what constitutes 'satisfactory performance', so that it could be interpreted quite widely. It also enhanced the risk that directors might be judged by short-term performance, with the result that they would focus on short-term share price values, rather on the longer-term profitability of their company.

- The report recommended **greater disclosures about the remuneration of individual directors**, including details of each component of their remuneration package, including share options, bonuses and pension contributions. There should also be disclosure of any service contract for a director with a notice period in excess of one year, and the reasons for the long notice period should be explained.

- To provide some accountability to the shareholders, it was recommended that shareholders should have access to the chairman of the remuneration committee at the annual general meeting, for questions and answers.

It is important to note that there is no question of the shareholders having any control over directors' remuneration, neither the remuneration of individuals nor the remuneration policy generally. The power to decide remuneration levels remains with the board, which is simply required to provide disclosures to shareholders, and allow them to ask questions at the AGM.

The report included **general recommendations about remuneration policy**, most of which are arguably open to broad interpretation.

- Executive pay should not be excessive. However, the remuneration committee should consider the wider pay scene when establishing its policy, and should offer remuneration packages that are sufficient to attract, retain and motivate individuals of the required quality. In effect, this means that a remuneration committee could justify virtually any package that it offers to a director on the grounds that it was necessary to attract a person of the necessary calibre.

- The performance-related elements of remuneration should reconcile the interests of the director with those of the shareholders. The performance criteria should be 'relevant, stretching and designed to enhance the business'. The remuneration committee is therefore required to give some thought to how this can be achieved in formulating its policy. The report gave some guidelines. Matters to consider should be the phasing of any reward schemes, the nature of any share option package and the implications of each element of the remuneration package for payments into the director's pension scheme. Setting upper limits on the award of bonuses should 'always be considered'.

- Where share options are granted as part of a remuneration scheme, they should not be issued at a discount. For example, suppose the current share price of ABC plc is 500 pence. If an executive director is granted share options as part of an incentive arrangement, the exercise price of the options should not be less than 500 pence. (Up to this time, it was quite usual to grant share options to directors at some discount to the current market price.)

- The granting of share options should be phased rather than in single large awards. It is better to make smaller awards frequently than large awards occasionally. Single large awards have the disadvantage of making the director concerned focus on the share price in the short term rather than the longer term. For example, suppose that a director is awarded 300,000 share options at an exercise price of 400 pence, which can be exercised after three years at the earliest and ten years at the latest. The temptation for the director would be to focus on what the share price will be as soon as the options can be exercised. In contrast, if the director is awarded 100,000 share options each year for three years, instead of 300,000 all at once, his interest in the share price will be longer-term.

Another issue addressed in the report was compensation payments to directors for loss of office. Remuneration committees were urged to take a firm line on the payment of compensation to directors who are dismissed for unsatisfactory performance. The reduction of notice periods in service contracts to 12 months should help to limit compensation payments, but when directors have very high salaries and share option and bonus arrangements, compensation for loss of office can still be very high. In the public perception, a high pay-off to an outgoing chief executive can look very much like a reward for failure.

The Greenbury report also suggested that the remuneration committee should give some thought to paying compensation over a period of time, instead of in a single lump sum, and to halt these periodic payments if the individual concerned takes up another job. However, the recommendations of the report about taking a tough line on compensation are more easily stated than applied, because the outgoing director has contractual rights in his or her service contract that the company should not breach.

Greenbury and amendments to the UK Listing Rules

The London Stock Exchange adopted the recommendations of Greenbury, and incorporated its recommendations into the UK Listing Rules, which currently contain the following requirements for listed companies incorporated in the UK.

The board must provide an annual report to the shareholders, containing a statement on the company's policy on directors' remuneration. The elements of remuneration for each individual director by name should be disclosed, including salaries and fees, annual bonuses, deferred bonuses, and compensation for loss of office. For each director by name, information should also be provided about share options and details of any other long-term incentive scheme other than share options. An explanation and justification should be provided for any element of remuneration that is pensionable, other than basic salary. The report should also include a statement on the company's policy for granting share options and other long-term incentive schemes, together with a justification for any departure from that policy in the period under review.

The detailed disclosures on directors' remuneration should be checked by the external auditors.

10.4   The Hampel Report

The Hampel Committee (the Committee on Corporate Governance) was set up in 1996 to carry out a review of the Cadbury Code and the Greenbury report, and to propose amendments where appropriate. It eventually reported in 1998.

The broad view of the committee was that it should recommend principles rather than prescriptive detailed regulations, and that the most suitable form of corporate governance will depend on the circumstances of the company. It condemned detailed regulations as box-ticking. 'Box-ticking takes no account of the diversity of circumstances and experiences among companies and within the same company over time.' Commenting on the assumptions that the roles of chairman and chief executive should always be kept separate, and that the notice period in service contracts should never exceed 12 months, the committee's report stated: 'We do not think there are universally valid answers on such points.'

In its introduction, the report also stated that whereas the Cadbury and Greenbury reports had been concerned mainly with preventing abuses, the Hampel committee was equally concerned with the positive benefits that could be obtained from best practice in corporate governance.

The report also stated clearly the view of the committee that the primary responsibility of the board of directors was towards the shareholders, and the task of the board should be to enhance the value of the shareholders' investment over time. Although there were other stakeholders, the directors had no responsibility towards these. The performance of the directors should therefore be judged exclusively on the basis of what they had achieved for the shareholders.

The Hampel report contained a list of principles of corporate governance, which are set out below. It is useful to note that, by their very nature, the principles are expressed in general terms, and avoid specific detail.

The directors

- A company should be headed by an **effective board**, to lead and control the company.

- The **two key tasks** at the top of each company are running the board and executive responsibility for running the company's business, tasks typically assigned to the chairman and chief executive. The report simply recommended that the company should explain publicly how these tasks are carried out. Where the tasks of chairman and chief executive are combined, a senior non-executive director should be identified.

- There should be a **balance on the board** between executive and non-executive directors, such that no individual or small group of individuals can dominate the board. Some of the non-executives should be independent.

- The board should be **supplied with information**, in a timely fashion, sufficient to enable it to discharge its duties properly.

- There should be a transparent and formal procedure for the **appointments to the board**. (This might involve the use of a nominations committee of the board.)

- All directors should submit themselves for **re-election at regular intervals**, and not less than once every three years.

Directors' remuneration

- The levels of remuneration for directors should be sufficient to attract and retain good people. The component parts of an individual's remuneration package should be structured so that rewards are linked to individual and company performance.

- A formal and transparent procedure should be established for developing company policy on directors' remuneration and deciding the remuneration for individual directors. No director should be involved in deciding his own remuneration.

- The company's annual report should contain a statement of remuneration policy and details of the remuneration of each individual director. However, the committee saw no need for this policy to be subject to a vote of approval by shareholders at the AGM (annual general meeting).

Shareholders

The Hampel report gave consideration to the relationship between a company and its shareholders, encouraging the idea of greater dialogue and communication. In return, shareholders were expected to make a greater contribution, partly by exercising what rights they have. Some of the recommendations in the report were directed at the common practice among many institutional investors of avoiding involvement with companies in which they held shares.

- Institutional investors should adopt a 'considered policy' on voting their shares.

- There should be a dialogue between a company and its institutional investors, based on a mutual understanding of objectives.

- When evaluating the corporate governance disclosures by a company, institutional investors should give due weight to all the relevant factors drawn to their attention in the information provided.

- Companies should use their annual general meeting to communicate with private shareholders, and encourage their participation.

Accountability and audit

The Hampel report repeated some of the recommendations of Cadbury.

- In its financial reports to shareholders, the board should present a balanced and understandable assessment of the company's position and prospects.

- The board should establish formal and transparent arrangements for maintaining an appropriate relationship with its external auditors.

- The external auditors should report independently to the shareholders. (As a result of the corporate governance requirements for listed companies, the auditors' report in the company's annual report and accounts was extended to include more than the statutory information.)

Significantly, the Hampel report reintroduced the recommendation originally made by Cadbury, and subsequently watered down, that the board should maintain a **sound system of internal control**, to safeguard the shareholders' investment and the company's assets. This responsibility applies to **internal controls generally,** not just to financial controls. **Board responsibility for risk management generally** was therefore established as 'best practice', six years after this suggestion had been made by the Cadbury committee.

10.5 The Combined Code

The Hampel Committee recommended that its recommendations should be combined with the Cadbury Code and the Greenbury recommendations to produce a single code of corporate governance for UK listed companies. With a few further amendments, the London Stock Exchange (which at the time was the authority for the Listing Rules in the UK) published the Principles of Good Governance and Code of Best Practice, more commonly known as the Combined Code.

As its longer title suggests, the Combined Code consists of two elements, both principles and a more detailed code of practice. The principles provide a conceptual framework and the code of practice indicates how the principles should be applied. For each principle, there are one or more supporting items in the code of practice.

The Code is also divided into two sections, a set of principles and a code of best practice for companies (Section 1 of the Combined Code) and a different set of principles and code of practice for institutional investors (Section 2 of the Code).

The Listing Rules were amended to require listed companies incorporated in the UK to include, in their annual report and accounts, a narrative statement of how they have applied the **principles** set out in section 1 of the Code, so that shareholders can evaluate how the principles have been applied. There should also be a statement of whether or not the company has complied during the period under review with the detailed provisions in the **code of best practice** in Section 1. A company that has not complied with all the provisions of the Code must specify which provisions it has not complied with, giving reasons.

The Code is not compulsory, but the requirement to explain each and every aspect of non-compliance is. Pressure from financial institutions on companies, together with the requirement for disclosure, has meant that in practice most listed companies now comply fully, or almost fully, with all the provisions of the Code.

The principles of good governance and code of best practice in detail

The Combined Code principles of good governance and code of best practice are set out below, with some comments. Where there is no change from the Cadbury Code, or the Greenbury Committee or Hampel Committee recommendations, no further comments are added.

Section 1 for companies divides the principles and the code into four broad categories, relating to the directors, directors' remuneration, relations with shareholders, and accountability and audit.

Directors

Principle

Every listed company should be headed by an effective board which should lead and control the company.

Code of best practice

The board should meet regularly and should have a formal schedule of matters of matters reserved to it for decision. All directors should bring an independent judgement to bear on issues of strategy, performance, resources (including key appointments) and standards of conduct. All directors should have access to professional advice where necessary, at the company's expense, for carrying out their duties. The code also includes a requirement that when an individual is first appointed to the board of a public company (and subsequently, as necessary), he or she should receive appropriate training.

There are two key tasks at the top of every public company (as explained earlier). The principle follows the Hampel recommendations by stating that 'there should be a clear division of responsibilities at the head of the company which will ensure a balance of power and authority, such that no one individual has unfettered powers of decision.' It does not state that the two positions should not be held by the same individual

In contrast, the code states on this point that a decision to combine the posts of chairman and chief executive in the same person must be publicly justified. Whether the two posts are held by one person or two different people, there should also be a strong and independent non-executive element on the board, with a recognized senior member other than the chairperson. (The chairman could hold the position in either an executive or non-executive capacity.) The recognized senior non-executive is someone 'to whom concerns can be conveyed.' The chairman, chief executive and senior non-executive should be identified in the company's annual report. This part of the Code establishes that in a situation where a company is having difficulties with its chairman and chief executive, investors will expect the senior non-executive to give other board colleagues a lead in dealing with the problem.

The board should include a balance of executive and non-executive directors, including independent non-executives, so that no individual or small group of individuals can dominate decision-taking by the board.

The board should include non-executives of 'sufficient calibre and number', so that they carry weight in decision-making by the board. The Code specifies that **non-executives should make up not less than one-third of the board**. The majority of the non-executives should be independent of the management and free from any business relationship (or other relationship) that could seriously affect their independence of judgement.

The board should be supplied with information in a timely manner, and in a form and of a quality sufficient to enable it to perform its duties properly.

Management is responsible for providing the information, but the directors should not rely on management to provide the management to provide the information needed in all circumstances. Directors should therefore make further enquiries where appropriate. The chairman should also make sure that the directors are properly briefed before board meetings. This is usually achieved in practice by issuing board papers in advance of the meeting.

There should be a formal and transparent procedure for new appointments to the board.

Unless the board is small, a **nominations committee** of the board should be established to make recommendations on new board appointments. The majority of the members of this nominations committee should be non-executive directors.

All directors should be required to submit themselves for re-election and at least once every three years.

Non-executives should be appointed for a specified term, subject to re-election. A newly-appointed director should be subject to election by shareholders at the first opportunity after their appointment (usually at the next AGM).

Directors' remuneration

Principle

'Levels of remuneration should be sufficient to attract and retain the directors needed to run the company successfully, but companies should avoid paying more than is necessary for this purpose. A proportion of executive directors' remuneration should be structured so as to link rewards to corporate and individual performance.'

Code of best practice

The remuneration committee should be 'sensitive to the wider scene', especially when deciding annual salary increases. It should also be aware of what comparable companies are paying and should take account of relative performance. However, the Code warns that comparisons should be used with caution, because there is a risk that they can result in result in an 'upward ratchet' in pay levels without any improvement in performance. The performance-related elements of the remuneration package of executive directors should form a significant part of their total remuneration, and 'should be designed to align their interests with those of shareholders and … give these directors keen incentives to perform at the highest levels.' The Code includes a schedule of provisions for designing a remuneration scheme. Share options should not be offered to directors at a discount. The board should set as an objective reducing the notice period for directors to one year or less, but should recognize that this might not be possible in the short term. It might also be necessary to offer a longer notice period to new directors recruited from outside the company. The Code also addresses the issue of compensation for early termination of a service contract (ie compensation for loss of office). The Code suggests methods of avoiding excessive pay-outs, but recognizes the possible legal constraints.

Companies should develop a formal and transparent procedure for developing a remuneration policy for executives and for fixing the remuneration packages of individual directors. No director should be involved in fixing his or her own remuneration.

To avoid potential conflicts of interest, there should be a remuneration committee of the board, consisting of independent non-executive directors. This should make recommendations to the board within agreed terms of reference, on the framework for executive remuneration. It should also decide the specific remuneration packages for each individual executive director. The board itself should decide the remuneration of the non-executive directors. (The shareholders should set the remuneration of non-executives if required by the articles of association.) The remuneration committee should consult with the chairman and chief executive about the remuneration of the other executive directors. The chairman should also ensure that the company maintains contact with its principal shareholders about directors' remuneration.

The company's annual report should contain a statement on remuneration policy and details of the remuneration of each director.

The Code includes provisions relating to the content of the remuneration report. The remuneration report need not be a standard item on the agenda at the company's AGM, but the board should consider each year whether shareholders should be invited to approve the policy in a vote at the AGM. However, shareholders should be invited specifically to approve any new long-term incentive scheme for directors.

Relations with shareholders

Principle

'Companies should be ready, where practicable, to enter into a dialogue with institutional shareholders base don the mutual understanding of objectives.' Boards should use the AGM to communicate with private investors and encourage their participation.

Code of best practice

There is no item in the code of best practice supporting the general principle. The Code, however, encourages both the company and institutional investors to engage in dialogue. Notice of the AGM and related papers papers should be sent out to shareholders at least 20 working days before the meeting. There should be a separate resolution at the AGM for each substantially separate issue, so that shareholders can vote on each issue independently. The chairman of the board should also ensure that the chairmen of the audit, remuneration and nominations committees are present at the AGM and available to answer questions.

Accountability and audit

Principle

The board should present a balanced and understandable assessment of the company's position and prospects.

Code of best practice

This calls for an assessment of **current** position and **future** prospects. This responsibility extends beyond the annual report and accounts, to the interim statement at the half-year stage and other price-sensitive public reports and reports to regulators. The directors should also report that the business is a going concern.

'The board should maintain a sound system of internal control to safeguard shareholders' investment and the company's assets.'

This requirement extends to all internal controls, not just internal financial controls. It assigns the ultimate responsibility for risk management to the board of directors. This is an important aspect of the combined Code, and is considered in more detail later. The code of best practice requires directors, at least annually, to carry out a review of the effectiveness of the internal control system within the group and report to shareholders that they have done so. This review should cover all controls, including financial, operational and compliance controls and risk management. Companies that do not have an internal audit unit should, from time to time, review the need for one.

The board should establish formal and transparent arrangements for considering how they should apply the financial reporting and internal audit principles of the combined Code, and for maintaining an appropriate relationship with the company's auditors.	The board should set up an audit committee consisting of at least three non-executive directors, with written terms of reference setting out its authority and duties. A majority of this committee should be independent non-executives. The duties of the committee should include keeping under review the scope and cost of the audit, and the independence and objectivity of the auditors. 'Where the auditors also supply a substantial volume of non-audit services, the committee should keep the nature and extent of such services under review, seeking to balance the maintenance of objectivity and value for money.'

The relationship between a company and its auditors and the independence and objectivity of the auditors are matters of considerable relevance to good practice in corporate governance. When US energy company Enron collapsed in 2001, press attention was drawn to the company's auditors, Andersen, and whether the impending financial problems of the company should have been signalled in the auditors' annual report. Some critics suspected that the audit firm was too close to the client company, taking large fees for non-audit work each year, such that it would be difficult for the audit work to be carried out with sufficient objectivity. Suggestions were also made that the auditors had agreed to questionable accounting practices by the company, and that investors relied on the 'clean bill of health' for the company in the audit report when the financial statements of the company were in fact unreliable.

In the UK, concerns arising out of the Enron affair led to various suggestions. One suggestion was that public companies should change their external auditors at least once every four years, to prevent a 'cosy' relationship building up. Another suggestion, by the Association of British Insurers, was that if a partner from the audit firm left his or her firm to join the board of a client company, the company should be obliged to switch to different external auditors.

Performance-related remuneration and the Combined Code recommendations

The remuneration of executive directors remains a problematical area for corporate governance. Although there is widespread public distaste for 'fat-cat directors' with very high remuneration, institutional investors are more concerned with encouraging directors to achieve performance targets that benefit the shareholders. High remuneration in itself is not a bad thing, as long as it is a reward for effective performance.

The Combined Code therefore specifies certain provisions on performance-related remuneration.

- If the remuneration committee considers that a director should be eligible for annual bonuses, performance conditions should be 'relevant, stretching and designed to enhance the business'. Upper limits on annual bonuses should always be considered, to prevent excessive payments.

- The remuneration committee should consider whether the directors should be eligible for benefits under long-term incentive schemes, such as share-option schemes. When share options are granted to directors, they should not normally be exercisable for at least three years from the date of their grant. Directors should also be encouraged to hold on to their shares for 'a further period' after the share options have been exercised.

- Any proposed new long-term incentive scheme should be approved by the shareholders, and should either replace existing schemes or form part of an overall incentives plan incorporating existing schemes.

- Pay-outs under all incentive schemes should be 'subject to performance criteria reflecting the company's objectives'. The selected performance criteria should perhaps involve a comparison with similar companies of key variables such as total shareholder return (TSR).

- If grants of share options are awarded in one large block rather than phased, the annual report of the remuneration committee should provide a justification.

- The remuneration committee should consider the pension consequences of changes to a director's remuneration. Annual bonuses should not normally be pensionable. If they are, a justification should be included in the annual report of the committee.

Institutional investors and the Combined Code

The Combined Code has a non-compulsory section (Section 2) containing principles and a code of best practice for institutional investors. The aim of these is to encourage institutions to take a more active role in the governance of companies in which they invest, by making sure that the board is properly accountable. This should be achieved by making their views known to the company.

The principles of governance for institutional investors are, firstly, that they should make 'considered use' of their votes. They should try to apply the same criteria of corporate governance to all the companies in which they invest, and should take steps to make sure that their voting intentions are turned into practice.

Institutional investors should also be ready to enter into a dialogue with companies based on 'the mutual understanding of objectives'. The Code does not go into detail about how this dialogue should be maintained, and it has been left to the associations of institutional investors, such as the Association of British Insurers (ABI) and the National Association of Pension funds (NAPF), to issue guidelines to their members.

10.6 The Turnbull Report and a risk-based approach to management

The requirement in the Combined Code for the board of directors to maintain a sound system of internal control was a new development in UK corporate governance, and listed companies wanted to know what this responsibility entailed. The Chartered Institute of Accountants in England and Wales (ICAEW) set up a committee, the Turnbull Committee, to provide guidelines for directors. The Turnbull report, *Internal Control: Guidance for Directors on the Combined Code*, was published in 1999 and had the support of the London Stock Exchange. It recommends a risk-based approach to designing, operating and maintaining a sound system of internal control.

The guidelines encourage the management of risk, not its elimination. A company with a low appetite for risk is unlikely to earn a sufficient rate of return in a competitive marketplace. Turnbull provides guidance in the form of a framework rather than detailed rules, so that each company can adapt the framework to suit its own particular circumstances. Instead of providing a list of controls that all companies should apply, it calls on boards of directors to identify risks that are significant in terms of achieving corporate objectives, and to implement a sound system of internal control. To do this, the board needs to be clear about what the company's objectives are. This calls for long-term strategic thinking. Some significant risks can be seen by taking a bird's eye view at senior management level within the group. Other significant risks are identified from detailed working knowledge. The task is to bring the two strands together.

The report also states that the board should establish a sound system for **reviewing the effectiveness of the system** of internal control, and that this should be part of embedded management and governance procedures within the company or group.

A sound system of internal controls contributes to corporate governance in three important ways:

- It facilitates effective and efficient operations, reducing the risk of losses through fraud and helping to ensure that the liabilities of the company (including 'off balance sheet items' such as guarantees and future commitments) are identified and managed.

- It also improves the reliability of internal and external reporting.

- It helps to ensure compliance with laws and regulations.

Risks facing a company are continually changing, therefore the system of internal controls should include a regular reassessment of the nature and scope of the risks facing the company. Profits are in part a reward for risk-taking, and the purpose of internal control is not to eliminate risk, but to help to manage and control it, so that the risks are acceptable in relation to the expected level of profits.

The board and management should consider all risks facing the company, not just financial risks. For example, with the globalization of markets and worldwide brands, together with the growing prominence of international pressure groups, many companies now find **reputation risk** a matter of significance. In this context, **environmental risk** is important. This can lead to large direct costs (remedial expenditure, fines) as well as severely damaging a firm's international reputation.

Responsibilities for risk management and internal controls

The Turnbull report specifies the respective responsibilities of the board of directors and management for internal controls.

The **board** has responsibility for the system of internal control and should set appropriate policies for this system. It should also carry out regular reviews to obtain reassurance that the system is functioning effectively. It should also ensure that the system of internal control it has established is effective in managing risks as intended and in the way the board has approved.

- Once a control strategy has been agreed, the **residual risk** remaining to the business can be assessed. To ensure that the board concentrates on areas that will yield the best results, it should focus on the limited number of risks where the residual risk is identified as being significant.

- Key risk indicators and the results of embedded monitoring should be regularly supplied to the board or a designated committee of the board.

- When there is a proposed acquisition, the directors should want to know whether a full risk analysis has been carried out as part of the due diligence process.

The board of directors as a whole has the responsibility for internal control, even when it delegates the task to a committee. It should not assume that embedded controls will operate satisfactorily, and so should receive and review regular reports on internal controls, for example from management or an internal audit department. The board should also carry out an annual assessment, for the purpose of making its report on internal control to shareholders in the annual report and accounts, to make sure that it has considered all significant aspects of internal controls for the period under review.

The role of **management** is to implement the board's policy on risk and control. Management should identify and evaluate the risks facing the company, because they are in a better position to do this than the directors, and should present their findings to the board for consideration. They should also design, operate and monitor the system for internal control, to implement board policy. The report urges open communication between management and the board on matters relating to internal controls, in particular where management has identified significant control failures or weaknesses.

The report emphasizes that a sound system of internal control reduces but does not eliminate the possibility of poor judgement in decision-making, human error, the deliberate circumvention of controls by employees, and decisions by management to override the controls. Nor does the system provide protection against unexpected circumstances arising. The system should therefore provide a reasonable but not an absolute assurance that the company will not be hindered from achieving its business objectives or from the orderly and legitimate conduct of its business.

Internal audit

The report does not state that companies should have an internal audit unit or department, but comments that an internal audit function can provide assurance and advice to the board on risk control. The Combined Code requires the board of a company without an internal audit function to review from time to time the need for one. Internal audit is considered further in the next chapter.

Carrying out an assessment of risks

Some guidance is given to the board on how to carry out an assessment of risks, by suggesting questions to which there ought to be satisfactory answers.

- Does the company have clear objectives and have these been communicated so as to provide effective direction to employees on risk management and control issues?

- Are significant risks assessed on an ongoing basis? Significant risks could relate to market risk (averse movements in market prices, including the company's share price), and credit, liquidity, technological, legal, health, safety and environmental and reputational risk, and business probity issues.

- Do management and others have a clear understanding of what risks are acceptable to the board?

- Does the board have a clear strategy for dealing with significant risks, and is there a policy on how to manage them?

- Do the company's culture and performance reward systems support the business objectives and risk management? Do senior management demonstrate through their actions as well as their policies a commitment to competence and integrity?

- Are authority, responsibility and accountability defined clearly, such that decisions are made and actions taken by the appropriate people?

- Does the company communicate to its employees what is expected of them, and the scope of their freedom to act?

- Are there embedded processes within the company for monitoring the effective application of policies, processes and activities relating to internal control and risk management? These could include regular confirmations by employees of compliance with controls, and reviews by the internal audit department or management.

The report states that what makes a sound system of internal control will vary according to the circumstances of the company, including its size. The factors to consider when assessing the sufficiency of controls include the nature and extent of the risks facing the company, the acceptable level for each risk, the probability of an adverse event occurring and its likely impact, and the costs of applying operational controls compared with the likely benefits to be obtained from them.

Reporting of risk

The Turnbull Report does not ask directors to discuss their main risks in the annual report, but to state that there is an ongoing process for identifying, evaluating and monitoring significant risks, and that this system is reviewed regularly by the board. To provide an insight into the extent of senior management commitment to risk management, the board should also summarize its process for reviewing the effectiveness of internal control.

10.7 Conclusion

Attitudes to corporate governance have changed over time, and will probably continue to change. The original concern was the risk to companies and their shareholders from tyrannical all-powerful chief executives. The main concern today is probably the risk of poor decision-making by the board of directors due to inadequate attention to controls and risk management.

Although a system of corporate governance for UK listed companies has been established by the Combined Code, questions could be raised about its effectiveness, and there will inevitably be problems with its application in practice. Nevertheless, the system has addressed key issues in corporate governance. Significantly, the Hampel Report, the Combined Code and the Turnbull report are all based on the view that good practice in corporate governance will bring positive benefits for companies. Corporate governance should not be regarded as an irksome system of compliance with rules.

The Combined Code as it currently stands is probably just one more step on the way towards the goal of better corporate governance, and other developments will probably occur over time. The next chapter looks in more detail at some corporate governance issues that have been raised, and are still perhaps insufficiently resolved.

11

GOOD PRACTICE IN CORPORATE GOVERNANCE

After reading this chapter, you should:

● Be able to explain a number of key issues in corporate governance.

Introduction

The previous chapter explains the issues in corporate governance in the context of how recommendations for best practice evolved in the UK. This chapter looks at some of those issues in more detail and some of the problems that perhaps remain unresolved. There are further comments in this chapter on a risk-based approach to management, although the views of the Turnbull committee are also reflected in the chapters on that subject earlier in the book.

11.1   The board's role in corporate governance

Every stakeholder in a company has some input to corporate governance, but the board of directors holds the key role. By law, it has powers to control the company although it has some accountability to shareholders. It should reserve the right to make certain decisions for the company, such as major capital expenditure decisions, and is responsible for internal controls and risk management. Although the responsibility for operational decisions is delegated to executive managers, these managers are accountable to the board for their performance.

The distinction between the board of directors and executive management is blurred in the UK, because some directors also hold executive positions. In principle, however, there is no reason why any executive director, apart from the chief executive, should sit on the board of a company.

The approach in practice of a board of directors to corporate governance can range anywhere along a spectrum from passive to active. When the board takes a passive role, membership of the board is largely ceremonial, and directors might do little more than turn up for meetings and collect a fee. In decision-making, they will be led by executive management and rubber-stamp management policies. In contrast, an active board will give a lead in setting objectives and will monitor the performance of management, in the interests of the shareholders. They will analyse and questions the activities of management, and insist on having sufficient information to perform their task. Not surprisingly, the consensus view of best practice on corporate governance is that the board should have an active role, without taking over responsibility for managing operations from executives.

In the 'Anglo-Saxon model' of corporate governance (ie the model supported by institutions in the so-called Anglo-Saxon countries, notably the USA and UK) the board of directors is responsible for directing corporate actions and directors are agents for the shareholders, whose task is to pursue the corporate objective of maximizing shareholder wealth. The more populist 'stakeholder theory', that the board has responsibilities to all stakeholders in the company, is seen as a misleading distraction, incapable of providing better governance. A stakeholder approach distracts attention for the shareholder wealth objective, undermining the private property of shareholders and allowing the board of directors to avoid accountability to any specific stakeholder group. Improvements in corporate governance can be achieved only through greater accountability to shareholders.

Not all Anglo-Saxon institutions subscribe fully to this shareholder-focussed model. For example, the US investment institution Calpers has stated that: 'a company's long-term sustainable value depends on a board's accountability to the company's owners, the quality of its management and the strength of its relationships with employees, suppliers and lenders.'

There has been some debate as to whether the system of corporate governance should be self-regulatory or subject to enforcement by legislation. In the UK, the weight of argument has been largely in favour of self-regulation, on the grounds that legislation leads to cumbersome bureaucracy and box-ticking, could stifle business creativity and in any case cannot guarantee corporate 'good behaviour'. Rules can often be circumvented or abused.

11.2 The board and relations with shareholders

Although risk management has emerged as a major element of corporate governance, other aspects of best practice should also be applied. As far as institutional investors are concerned, the most important elements of good practice are probably accountability of the board to shareholders, openness in communications and minimizing conflicts of interest by aligning remuneration for directors as closely as possible with the achievement of the company's objectives. In the UK, the Myners Committee, set up by the Department of Trade and Industry to investigate how companies and institutional investors could work more closely together, made a number of recommendations in its report (2001). It suggested that the ideal or model company management is one that has clear objectives for the company, a strategy for achieving these objectives, a financing policy and capital expenditure and revenue plans, all of which it communicates annually to institutional investors and brokers. Management will also arrange regular meetings with shareholders to discuss long-term issues facing the company. In addition, it will have a clearly defined and articulated policy for the remuneration of executive directors that it also discusses openly with shareholders.

Corporate governance is an issue for all countries with capital markets. The OECD has issued a set of corporate governance principles, and the financial authorities in a number of countries have published codes of best practice. The concerns of institutional investors are perhaps best summarized by a ten-point code of corporate governance drawn up by the International Corporate Governance Network, an unofficial international association of investors.

1.   Companies should provide an optimal return to their shareholders.

2.   There should be accurate, adequate and timely disclosures of information.

3.   One share, one vote.

4.   The board should be accountable to shareholders.

5.   The remuneration of executives should be aligned to shareholder interests.

6.   Major modifications should not be made without shareholder approval.

7.   Corporate governance should focus on optimizing company performance.

8.   Governance should also focus on optimizing the return to shareholders.

9.   Companies to adhere to the laws of the countries in which they operate.

10. Any code of corporate governance should be followed pragmatically, rather than with a rigid 'box-ticking' approach to following the rules.

In spite of the demand from institutional investors for greater openness and accountability, actual practice still eaves much to be desired. The *Financial Times* (1 October 2001) reported a survey commissioned by World Investor Link, an investor relations specialist, into 200 of the top 500 European countries. The survey found that 10% of the companies surveyed did not know the identity of their top 50 shareholders, and that about a quarter of chief executives had met fewer than half of their top 50 shareholders during the previous six months.

11.3   The role of non-executive directors

A distinction should be made between non-executive directors generally and **independent** non-executive directors. Some directors are not independent. In public companies, the most frequent types of non-independent non-executive are probably:

●   Former executive directors who no longer have executive responsibilities, but who are appointed to the board in a non-executive capacity on retirement. These individuals often continue to identify with their executive colleagues.

●   Individuals who are appointed as representatives of a major shareholder, whose interests they will represent.

Independent non-executive directors are supposed to bring an independent view to the deliberations of the board, but they are in a fairly difficult position.

- As directors, they have fiduciary duties and the duty of skill and care, are they are legally liable in the same way as executive directors.

- As fellow directors, they might also be reluctant to 'blow the whistle' on their colleagues.

- Where they have been selected and appointed by the chairman or the chief executive officer, they could be less likely to ask tough questions about the way the company is being run. (This is sometimes known as the St Thomas à Becket problem, after the 12th-century Archbishop of Canterbury who was appointed to his position by the king, but then took a stance against the king on issues concerning the governance of the country.)

Non-executives face the further problem that they are required to join with their executive colleagues in making decisions for the company, for example on major new capital investments. However, they lack the 'insider knowledge' of executive managers about the business operations, and rely on the integrity of the information supplied to them by management and executive directors. Their scope for meaningful contribution to board decisions can therefore be limited.

In the UK, there has been strong criticism of independent non-executive directors, on the grounds that they do not fulfil their role adequately. For example, in February 2002, Paul Myners, author of a government-backed report into pension fund investment and former head of Gartmore Investment Management, the institutional investment firm, commented that in his view, boards were a 'self-perpetuating oligarchy' which failed to stand up for shareholders' rights against over-mighty executives. He called non-executives the 'missing link' in the chain of good corporate governance.

- Some individuals were non-executive directors of a large number of public companies, more than they could possibly serve effectively.

- Non-executive directorships are frequently given to the executive directors of other listed companies. This has given rise to concerns that non-executives will not ask difficult questions or take a stand against executives on the board, provided that the non-executives of his or her own company would be similarly lenient to them.

- Non-executives are appointed to make the board more accountable to the shareholders, but shareholders have opportunities to discuss the company with the non-executives only in a formal setting. The chairmen of the board committees are made available for questions at the annual general meeting. Any other discussions between shareholders and non-executives are informal, and might not take place at all.

- The law makes no distinction between executive and non-executive directors. In principle, the non-executives could be equally liable with the executives for negligence and failure to perform their fiduciary duties and duties of skill and care. It could be argued that this could make non-executives more inclined to support their executive colleagues.

It is instructive to look at some of these criticisms in more detail. Paul Myners was reported (*Observer*, 17 March 2002) as criticizing the system in many listed companies of making non-executive appointments, and argued for a more rigorous system of appointments. 'We have not pressed the independence of the nomination process hard enough. Boards tend to feel comfortable with someone who they know, someone who they feel comfortable with.' 'Nomination committees need to operate more effectively. Its chairman needs to be able to say to colleague how he sees the board operating, which skills and competences are required. The committee then needs to work with an external agency... to provide an objective list of candidates. Then interviews need to be held.'

The same *Observer* article reported a check carried out on the top 350 UK companies, which revealed that there were 80 individuals the report labelled as 'serial directors', ie individuals holding at least three directorships in the top 350 companies. Six of these 80 individuals held five top 350 director positions and 15 held four. Many of them also had seats on the boards of smaller companies, and some individuals had as many as 17 company directorships. The emphasis of the article was that a small number of individuals can start to wield a large amount of influence from the various positions they hold. It would also be argued that there must be a limit to the number of positions an individual can hold and still do the job properly.

11.4 The importance of risk management to companies

The Cadbury committee described risk management as 'the process by which executive management, under board supervision, identifies the risk arising from business ... and establishes the priorities for control and particular objectives.' In the committee's view, risk management should be systematic and embedded in the company's procedures and culture, and should not be *ad hoc* and occasional.

The importance of risk management for a company, as the previous chapters have established, is that a failure to control and contain risks could lead to financial collapse and the demise of the company.

Good management practices generally

The effective management of risk calls for the application of management principles that apply in general to the running of a company.

- Management should set objectives for the company, including objectives for the management of risk, and should plan how to achieve those objectives, monitor actual performance and, if possible, take control action where actual performance is below expectation.

- The authority for taking decisions and carrying out actions, together with responsibility and accountability, should be assigned to appropriate people. There should be no authority without responsibility or accountability. Equally, no one should be responsible for something over which he or she has no authority.

- There should be open communication of objectives, policies and plans and information about actual performance.

- Rewards to management and other employees should be based on performance, and performance should be judged in terms of the achievement corporate objectives.

Principles for effective risk management

There are three basic elements to effective risk management: identification, evaluation and control.

There has to be a mechanism or procedure for regularly reviewing the risks facing a company, to identify what they are. Risks change over time. Just one example is the reassessment of risks by the US banks Morgan Stanley and Goldman Sachs following the terrorist attack on the World Trade Centre in New York on 11 September 2001. These banks were reported (*Financial Times*, 25 January 2002) to be planning to move significant operations out of the lower Manhattan financial district. The terrorist attack had exposed flaws in their contingency plans, because too many of their operations had been located in a 'campus' area, sharing the same telecommunications and power grids. Morgan Stanley was reported to be moving some operations to the suburbs north of New York City and Goldman Sachs to be moving its equities business across the Hudson River to New Jersey.

The methods for **identifying risks** will vary according to the nature of the company and the risks. Financial risks can be identified by internal audit programmes, whereas hazard and operability studies (HAZOPS) might be used to identify physical and procedural hazards, and environmental audit programmes should be used to assess environmental risk.

The **evaluation of risks** calls for the application of risk measurement and ranking methods, such as quantified risk assessment.

Control systems need to be established both for monitoring risks and for identifying situations that are getting out of control or where an adverse event has occurred or might soon occur. Embedded control systems should be overlaid by a review system, to ensure that the control system is functioning effectively. The Turnbull report makes the board of directors responsible for carrying out such reviews regularly.

In January 2002, it was reported that activities by a rogue foreign exchange trader in the USA had led to losses of about $750 million for Allied Irish Bank. An incident of this kind obviously raised questions about the effectiveness of control system, and an important question for the bank would have been whether the control system itself, for preventing unauthorized trading by dealers, was sufficiently strong. If the control system was found to be adequate, the next question would be how did it fail in the case of the rogue trader. The failure could have been due to faults of management in not applying the controls properly, or in deliberate deceit by an employee who was able to hide the nature of his trading positions from his superiors. The failure might also have been due to a combination of factors.

Effective risk management depends on establishing a robust system of controls and making sure that these are applied and checked by management.

Corporate risk management policy

Effective risk management could be described as an application of principles of good management and sound management practices, but taking a pessimistic view of potential outcomes.

Decision-making should consider the risks as well as the benefits and returns. For example, all proposed capital investment projects should be assessed methodically against potential risks before financial authorization for the project is granted.

A risk management framework has the following requirements.

- There should be a clear and coherent risk strategy, and policies and standards for applying this strategy.

- There need to be arrangements for communicating and discussing risk and the control of risk. There should also be two-way communication within the organization, between senior management and others, to ensure that the company's risk management policies are properly understood and that the actual position is reported in order to assess how effectively the policies are being applied.

- The responsibilities for risk and the authority to manage it should be clearly defined and assigned to key staff.

- Within the company, there should be suitable risk programmes and procedures for the control of each significant aspect of risk.

- There should be suitable arrangements in place for monitoring and reviewing the management of risk. Not least, a company must demonstrate to itself that it is capable of learning from its own mistakes.

Functional responsibilities for risk management and coordination

The primary responsibility for operational risks lies with the line managers, who should be accountable to the board of directors. A system for monitoring and reporting risks should be established, and in large organizations this could involve appointing a risk manager for each division in the company and a senior risk manager for the company as a whole, with a direct reporting line either to the board of directors. The risk managers would be responsible for gathering information about risk, and possibly for drawing up a risk-management plan for the company and monitoring its implementation.

A risk manager for the company should ideally report to the board as a whole, or to the audit committee of the board, rather than to a particular individual director (such as the chief executive officer or the finance director). In practice, however, the risk manager might report to the CEO or the finance director.

The role of internal audit

The Combined Code in the UK requires the board of directors to review from time to time the benefits of having an internal audit function or department, if the company does not already have one. An internal audit function would act independently of executive managers, and would report either to the board itself, the audit committee, the chief executive officer or the finance director.

Traditionally, an internal audit department has carried out checks on the financial controls within a company, usually in collaboration with the external auditors. The main checks would be to make sure that suitable controls exist and are applied properly. In addition, internal auditors might conduct special investigations into particular aspects of the company's operations.

The department could also be more involved in risk management generally, providing continuous support to the risk-management process. For example, an internal auditor might participate in a risk oversight committee, with responsibility for the oversight and reporting of risks. The internal audit department might even take on the general function of risk management within the company, to coordinate risk-management activities, and monitor and report risks on a company-wide basis.

Internal auditors should bring objectivity to their role, which line managers cannot (because the 'blame' for control failures will often lie with line management). However, it is not the function of internal auditors to **manage** risks, only to monitor and report them, and to check that risk controls are efficient and cost-effective.

An internal audit investigation into internal controls and risk management should consider:

- the extent to which corporate objectives have been communicated at all levels and are supported by consistent business strategies, plans and targets

- the adequacy of the mechanisms for identifying, assessing and controlling significant business and financial risks, arising from both internal and external sources

- whether the company could react to dramatic one-off events that might threaten its ability to achieve its objectives.

Conclusion

This chapter has discussed issues that were current at the time of writing. It cannot be stressed enough, however, how much corporate governance issues are 'alive' and how recommended practice is likely to develop still further over time. It is a fascinating area, and you should keep an eye on the business and financial news.

INDEX